Raw-Edge Appliqué

14 Fast and Fun Frayed Quilt Projects

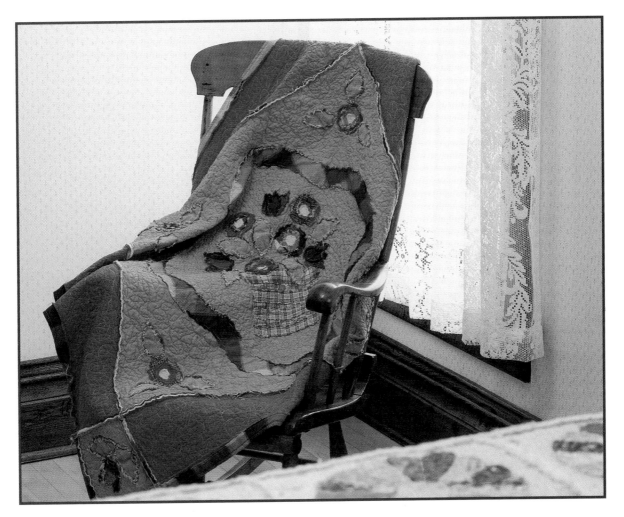

Jodie Davis

Published by

krause
publications
700 East State Street • Iola, WI 54990-0001
715/445-2214 • FAX: 715/445-4087   www.krause.com

Please call or write for our free catalog of publications. Our toll-free number to place an order or obtain a free catalog is (800) 258-0929.

Library of Congress Catalog Number: 2001097832
ISBN: 0-87349-332-X

Photography by Krause Publications.

Illustrations by Barbara Hennig, with quilt designs and patterns by Jodie Davis.

Dedication

To my friends cum sisters of Bee-Attitudes...
Sherrie Bowden, Joyce Brannon, Rebecca
Coffee, Lillian Cole, Carol Haas, Claudia Litton,
Gwynne Maffet, Clair McGuggey, Marilyn
Stafford, Jennie Suter, Jennifer Yacola, and
Valerie Yingling
... for helping me with all those "What to do
next?" questions and for their monthly dose of
general grounding and inspiration.

Table of Contents

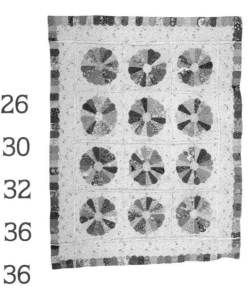
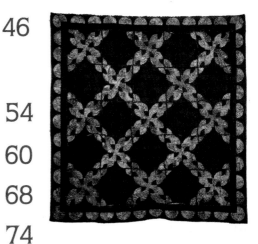
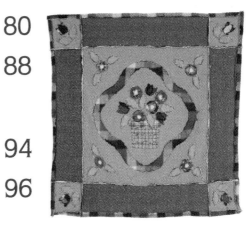

Acknowledgments

My gratitude to Barbara Hennig, whose lovely illustrations make my words virtually unnecessary.

Thanks to Glenda Irvine once again for her long-arm quilting skills; this time on Climbing Rose Log Cabin.

Thanks to the folks at The Warm Company for their great batting, to Classic Cottons for the fabric for Drunkard's Path, Madeira for the wonderful thread for Drunkard's Path, to Westfalenstoffe for the fabrics for Flower Baskets, and YLI for their Colours quilting thread for Boston Uncommon.

To everyone at Krause—my editor Maria Turner and page designer Donna Mummery, as well as Don Gulbrandsen and Brenda Mazemke—thanks for making the creation of this book such a pleasure and for making me look so good!

Hugs to my Bernina for yet another year full of happy hours spent humming along.

Preface

Why Raw-Edge Appliqué?

In the early 1990s, I wrote a book entitled *Three-Dimensional Appliqué*. One of the quilts showcased in that book was the Frayed Log Cabin design that also appears in this book.

Recently, observing the popularity of shaggy flannel quilts with snipped seam allowances, I decided it was time to explore the possibilities of this idea further.

And am I glad I did!

Making the quilts in this book has been immense fun. Raw-edge appliqué makes both old and new patterns fast and fun. And, best yet, because those loose raw edges cover joins, no one will see whether your points match up.

Easy, quick, snuggly quilts, and precision optional—sounds like a quilter's dream come true!

Introduction

What is Raw-Edge Appliqué?

Simply put, raw-edge appliqué is exactly that; patches are sewn down to a quilt top, leaving the raw edges exposed.

But there's more.

As you will see from the quilts in this book, I have applied this technique to both traditionally pieced and appliquéd designs. Imagine making an Orange Peel or Drunkard's Path quilt without sewing curved seams. Or a lovely trellised vine of roses without a stitch of needle turn. And if you're stitching isn't just right, so what, it won't show!

How Is It Done?

Raw-edge appliqué is as easy as laying down a fabric shape on a piece of background fabric and machine stitching ⅛" to ½" in from the raw edge. That's all there is to it. Really!

For more specifics, let's look at the Frayed Log Cabin quilt. You will have cut strips and marked your quilt top with the log cabin blocks. The idea here is to sew the strips or "logs" to the quilt top, leaving a ½" seam allowance all the way around. Thus, the 1" difference between the markings on the quilt top and the size of the log strips to be appliquéd.

You will pin a log to the quilt top, lining up the markings you made on the quilt top with the imaginary seam line on the logs, and sew the logs to the top ½" in from the raw edges. Of course, you can mark the seam line on the logs, but this is not at all necessary. (See illustration at left.)

When the quilt is complete no one will be able to see if your corners don't match because the seam allowances will be covering where the stitching meets. Remember: Accuracy isn't necessary with raw-edge appliqué!

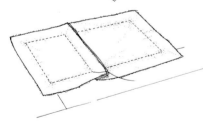

Center the first "log" over the markings for log 1 and stitch ½" from the raw edge. The stiching will be on the marked line on the quilt top.

Log Cabin is traditionally a pieced block.

The Orange Peel is constructed in the same way. (See illustration and close-up photo at right.)

You are probably wondering how I chose what seam allowance to use. That's easy. For some quilts, such as the Frayed Log Cabin, I wanted a lot of fraying and a fuzzy look; therefore, I cut my strips with an extra ½" all around.

Orange Peel is traditionally an appliquéd design.

In contrast, for Dressed to Bark, I didn't want to obscure the design of the doggies, as shown in the photo at right, so I chose a small seam allowance of ⅛".

Of course, you can adjust the seam allowances on the patterns to suit your taste.

Do you see why I call this painless quilt-making?

Detail of the Dressed to Bark design, which shows that any appliqué design can be raw-edge appliquéd.

Construction Choices

The raw-edge appliqué method opens up several quilt construction choices.

First, you can go the traditional route by sewing your quilt top first, then layer, quilt, and bind. Examples of this technique are the Climbing Rose Log Cabin and Orange Peel designs.

Or, a second option is to appliqué and quilt each block individually, and then sew them together into a quilt. Flower Basket and Drunkard's Path are made this way. Working on the blocks and border pieces before they are sewn together makes machine-quilting sweat-free without the bulk of an entire quilt to wrestle with. (Note that with this method where the blocks and border sections are joined, they were sewn with the backing fabrics

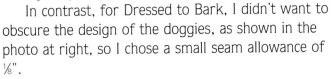

Drunkard's Path is traditionally a pieced design.

facing, so the seam allowances show on the front side of the quilt.)

The third and fastest method is the one I used for Frayed Log Cabin. I raw-edge appliquéd the fabric strip "logs" and quilted through the layers of the quilt sandwich all at one time in quilt-as-you-go fashion.

At the opposite end of the spectrum is Rose Log Cabin, which, other than the appliqué method, was constructed along conventional lines. I constructed the log cabin blocks with the paper-piecing method, then joined the blocks in Courthouse Steps style, and sewed the plain strips in between the block strips. Next, I raw-edge appliquéd the flowers, vines, and leaves to the top and added the borders. Then, I sent it to Glenda to be machine-quilted.

Climbing Rose Log Cabin is made by paper-piecing the logs, joining the blocks in Courthouse Steps style, and adding the raw-edge appliquéd flowers, vines, and leaves.

Wash Your Quilt!

Your raw-edge appliqué quilt isn't finished until you run it through the washer and dryer. Your laundry room completes the quilt by fraying those raw edges, giving the quilt that "cuddle me" look.

Detail of the raw-edge appliqué from the Flower Baskets design, showing before washing (above) and after (right).

Some of the quilts look just right after one cycle; others need a little more help fraying and will ask to be run through again.

Washing will shrink the quilt a bit, adding to that old-fashioned homey look. Using unwashed fabrics and an all-cotton batting, I find that my quilts have shrunk about 3 percent.

Basic
Quilt-
Making
Skills

Part One

Transferring the Patterns

To reproduce the patterns, trace or photocopy them from this book.

If you choose to use a photocopy machine to reproduce the patterns, watch out for distortion. To test the precision of the copy machine, make one copy of the block and measure it to be sure the size matches that of the original.

Basics of Rotary Cutting

As one who started quilting before the advent of the rotary cutter, I am thankful to whomever invented it each and every time I pick one up. Although it doesn't apply to every cutting job in quilt-making, it speeds up about 90 percent of it.

For the purposes of the projects in this book, we use elementary rotary cutting methods to cut strips and squares.

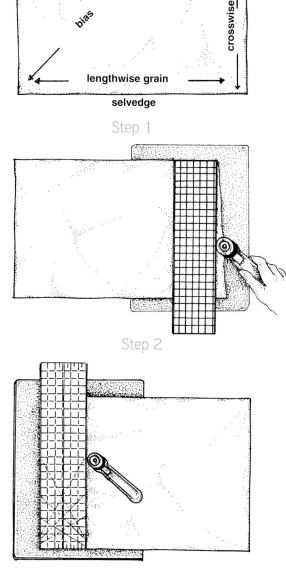

Step 1

Step 2

Step 3

1 You will notice that your fabric has two edges, one of which may have printing on it. These are the selvedges, and they run along the lengthwise grain of the fabric.

2 To prepare your fabric for rotary cutting, fold the fabric on your rotary cutting mat, matching the selvedge edges and having the fold away from you. Place the ruler's short side along the fold, and start cutting away from you, along the right-hand side of the ruler. (Left-handed quilters can reverse these instructions.)

3 Move to the other side of the table or move your mat, fabric, and ruler. Slide the ruler over the marking for the measurement you desire. Cut your strip.

4 To make squares or rectangles, place your fabric strip on the cutting mat crosswise. Line up the top edge of the ruler along the long top raw edge of the strip, and position the desired measurement marking with the short raw edge of the strip. Cut.

Mitered Borders

1 Measure the width and length of the quilt top through the center, subtracting out ½" for the seam allowances. Mark each border strip with pins, placing one at the center and one at each end to mark half the length of the measurements in step 1.

2 Pin a border strip to a corresponding side of the quilt top, matching the centers and corners.

3 Beginning and ending with a backstitch ¼" from the edge of the quilt top, stitch the border piece to the quilt top.

4 Repeat for the three remaining border pieces.

5 With right sides together, fold the quilt diagonally so that the border strips are aligned. Using a ruler with a 45-degree angle, draw a line on the wrong side of the border strip from the end of the stitching to the outside edge. Stitch exactly along the line. Trim the extra tails to ¼" and press.

6 Repeat for the three remaining corners.

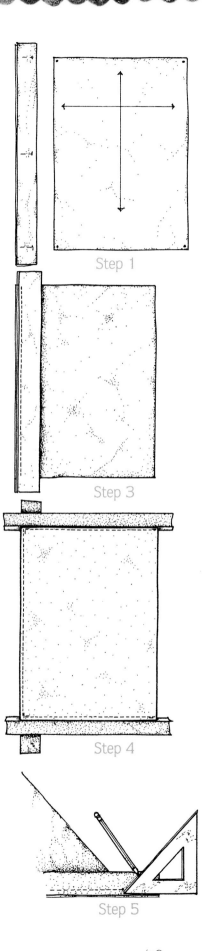

Step 1

Step 3

Step 4

Step 5

Preparing For Quilting

I have included a close-up photo of each of the quilts within the project instructions to show you how I quilted it. Of course, you should feel free to use whatever quilting design you prefer.

Before you begin to quilt, prepare your quilt by marking the top with the quilting design (although all of the quilts were quilted free-form, with no marked lines) and layering it with backing and batting. Follow steps 1 through 4 to prepare your quilt and steps 5 and 6 for quilting.

1 Mark the quilt top with the desired quilting design. I often trace my design onto freezer paper, which I iron in place to my quilt and then, carefully tear the paper away after quilting. It takes patience to tear without pulling stitches, but I prefer it to marking.

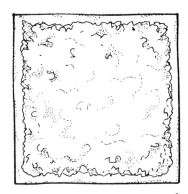

2 Cut the batting and backing 8" larger than the quilt top. This will give you 4" extra on each side of the quilt, which is the minimum a long-arm quilter requires.

3 Lay the backing, wrong side up, on a flat surface. Place the batting over the backing. Center the quilt top, right-side up, on top of the batting and backing.

Step 3

4 Working from the center out, baste the three layers of the quilt "sandwich" together with thread or safety pins.

5 Quilt the top as desired or as indicated in the project directions.

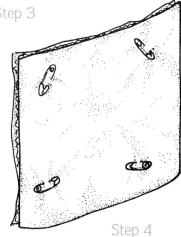

6 When you are finished quilting, remove all basting stitches or any remaining safety pins.

Step 4

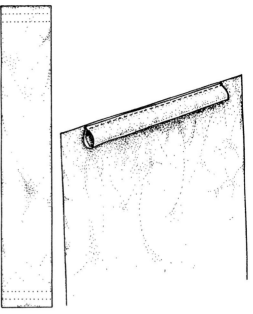

Quilt Sleeves

To easily hang your quilt on a wall, sew a simple sleeve to the back. For support, cut a ⅜" or ¾" dowel 1" to 2" longer than the sleeve.

Here's how to make your sleeve:

1 Cut a strip of fabric 6" wide and approximately 2" shorter than the width of the top edge of the quilt. Press less than ¼" at each short edge twice. Topstitch.

2 Right sides facing, fold the sleeve strip in half lengthwise. Press. Aligning the raw edge of the strip with the top raw edge of the quilt, baste the strip in place.

3 Stitch the binding to the quilt as instructed below, securing the sleeve in the seam.

4 Slipstitch the bottom folded edge of the sleeve to the back of the quilt.

5 Insert the rod and use nails in the wall to hang your quilt.

Step 1   Step 3

Step 4

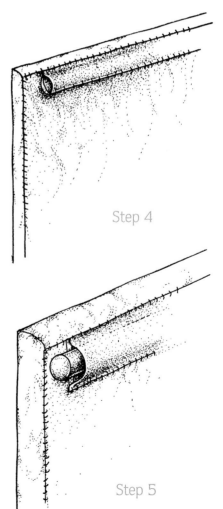

Step 5

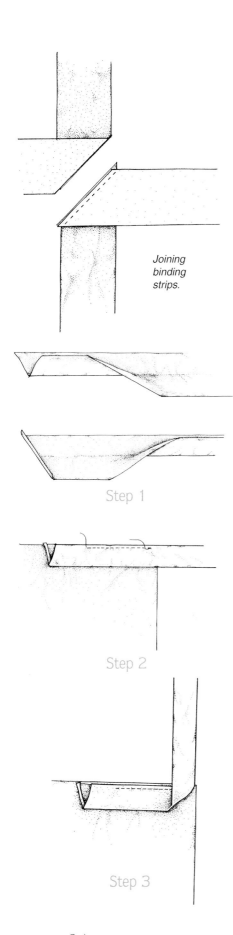

Joining binding strips.

Step 1

Step 2

Step 3

Making and Applying Binding

For all of the quilts in this book I have used 2½" binding strips cut on the straight of the grain. The only time I use bias is on curved edges. If you desire bias binding, be sure to purchase extra fabric.

For straight-grain binding, simply cut strips from the lengthwise or crosswise grain of the fabric. Join the ends together to make one long, continuous strip.

1 Trim the batting and backing even with the quilt top. With wrong sides together, press the binding strip in half lengthwise.

2 Place the binding strip along one edge of the right side of the quilt top, matching raw edges. Leaving the first 6" or so of the binding free, stitch the binding to the quilt. Use a ¼" seam allowance. Stop stitching ¼" from the corner. Backstitch and remove the quilt from the machine.

3 Turn the quilt to prepare to sew the next edge. Fold the binding straight up, creating a 45-degree angle fold.

4 Fold the binding down, having the fold even with the top edge of the quilt and the raw edge aligned with the side of the quilt. Beginning at the edge, stitch the binding to the quilt, stopping ¼" from the next corner.

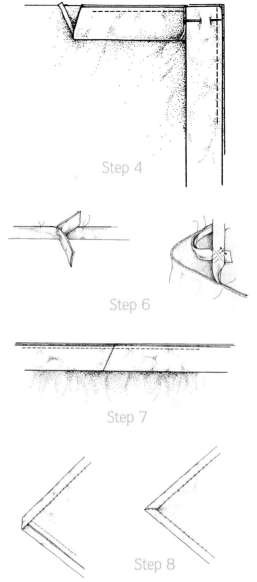

Step 4

5 Backstitch and remove the quilt from the machine. Continue the folding and stitching process for the remaining corners.

Step 6

6 When you are within approximately 8" of the starting point, stop stitching. Overlap the ends of the binding and mark them with matching pins. Clip the binding raw edges at the pin marks, being careful not to cut past the seam allowance or into the quilt layers.

Open up the binding and match the ends as shown. Stitch the ends together on the diagonal.

Step 7

7 Check to be sure that the binding fits the quilt. Trim off the binding tails and finish stitching the binding to the edge.

8 Fold the binding to the back of the quilt over the raw edges of the quilt "sandwich," covering the machine stitching. Slipstitch the binding in place, mitering the corners.

Step 8

The Projects

Please note that I've arranged the quilts according to appliquéd designs vs. pieced. Instructions for the appliquéd variations (Flower Baskets, Baskets Full of Kitties, Dressed to Bark, and Climbing Rose Log Cabin) appear first, followed by the pieced designs (Dresden Plate, Frayed Log Cabin, Boston Uncommon, American Lone Star, Drunkard's Path, and Orange Peel).

Part Two

Flower Baskets

The marriage of the raw-edge technique and the warm country look of the German Westfalenstoffe fabrics is a winning combination in this quilt.

The appliqués are sewn to the sections of the quilt, the sections are quilted, and then the sections are sewn together with the seam allowances to the front.

To make an easy binding, the backing is cut 1½" larger on the outside edge than the batting and front of the quilt and is then folded over to the front and topstitched in place as the last step of the construction.

Finished Size

48" square before washing

Materials

¼-yard green leaf fabric
⅛-yard each of two plaid fabrics for basket
Fat quarters or scraps of six fabrics to mix and match for flowers
Scrap of yellow for flower centers
1 yard lighter pink fabric for center background and border corners
1 yard darker pink fabric for borders
2 yards backing fabric
2 yards batting
Quilting thread

Cutting Plan

Cut a 32½" square for the center background from the pink fabric.
Cut four 9½" x 9½" light pink background fabric squares for border corners.
Cut four 9½" x 32½" dark pink pieces for side borders.
Cut backing into:
  One 32½"
  Four 9½" x 9½"
  Four 9½" x 32½"
Cut batting into:
  One 32½" square
  Four 8¼" x 32½" for border sides
  Four 8¼" squares for border corners
Cut the appliqués as instructed on patterns, pages 22-23.

Instructions

1 Arrange the appliqués on the center background square and border corner sections.

Raw-edge appliqué them in place by stitching ¼" from the raw edges. Refer to the quilt layout at left for placement.

Step 1
Flower Baskets Quilt Layout

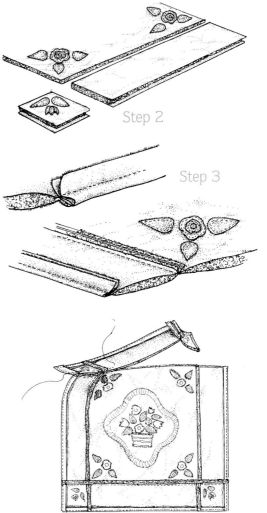

Step 2

Step 3

Step 4

Step 5

2 Layer and quilt each section of the quilt: the center section, four side border sections, and the four corners. For the borders and corners, place the batting so it butts against one long side of the fabric.

3 Fold the backing and quilt top at the outside edges of each border piece 1¼" to the front of the quilt for each border section.

4 Topstitch in place with your quilting thread, ¼" from the folded edge.

5 Backing sides facing, stitch two side border pieces to the sides of the center section. Stitch the corner sections to the ends of the two remaining border sections. Stitch these border sections to the top and bottom of the quilt.

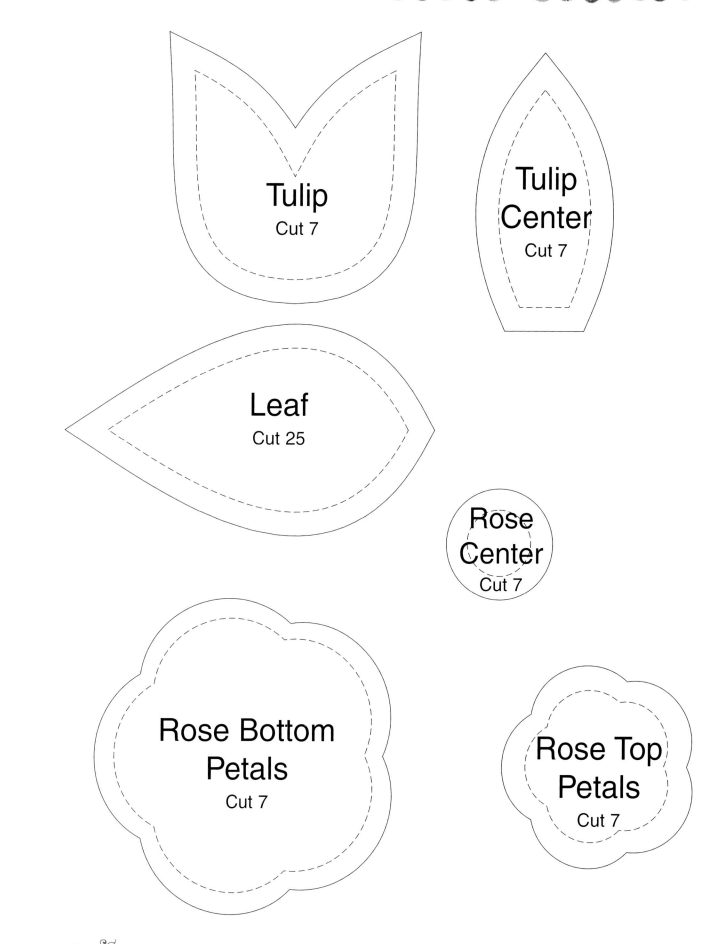

Tulip
Cut 7

Tulip
Center
Cut 7

Leaf
Cut 25

Rose
Center
Cut 7

Rose Bottom
Petals
Cut 7

Rose Top
Petals
Cut 7

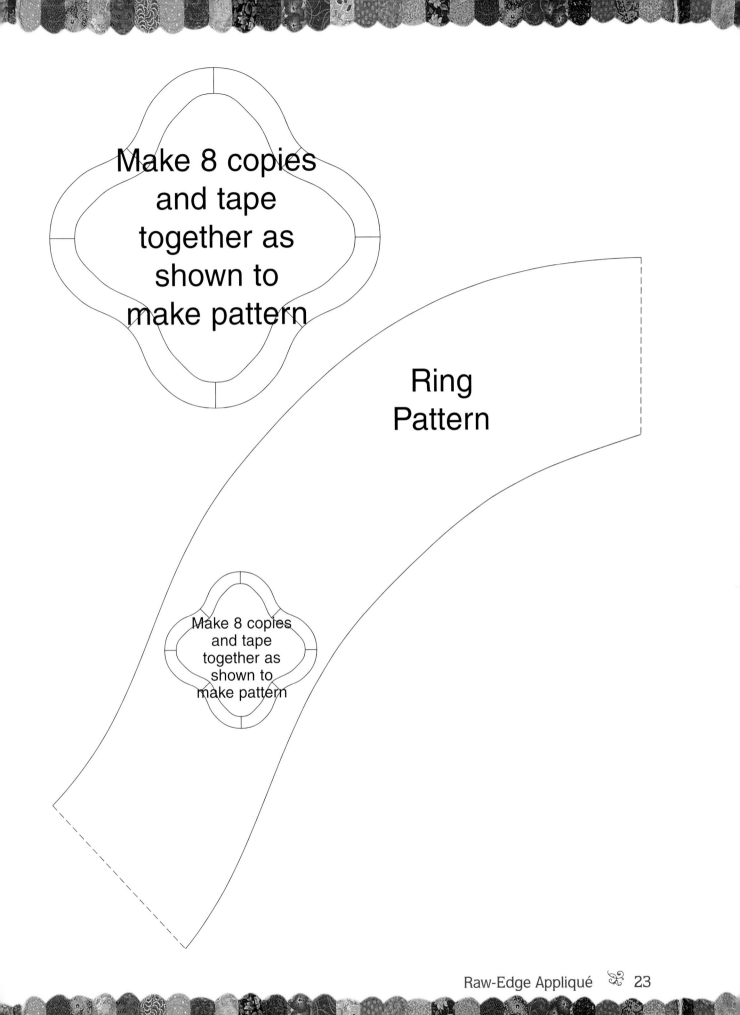

Make 8 copies
and tape
together as
shown to
make pattern

Ring
Pattern

Make 8 copies
and tape
together as
shown to
make pattern

Flower Baskets Placemats

Raw-edge appliqué is perfect for everyday use—and not only on beds and laps. Stitch up a set of easy-care quilted wear for your table with this placemat variation to the Flower Baskets quilt design.

Finished Size

14" x 18" before washing

Materials

14" x 18" placemat foundation fabric
14" x 18" placemat backing fabric
10" x 14" fabric for flower background

Scraps of fabric for the three parts of the flower and the leaves
13" x 17" batting
Quilting thread
Basting spray (optional)

Cutting Plan

Cut two leaves and one each of the three parts of the rose on page 28.

Instructions

1 Arrange the three layers of the placemat starting with backing fabric right-side down, then center the batting on the wrong side of the backing, and place the foundation fabric right-side up on top of the batting, matching the raw edges with those of the backing fabric.

2 Add the background rectangle on top, centering it. Pin the layers together or use the basting spray as you layer.

3 Referring to the project layout, arrange the leaves and the bottom, larger, piece of the flower on the foundation fabric. Pin.

4 Using the quilting thread, stitch ¼" in from the raw edges of the pieces. Add and do the same for the two remaining pieces of the flower.

5 Stitch ½" from the raw edges all the way around the outside of the flower background and the placemat.

6 Quilt the placemat as shown at right, or in your own design.

7 Wash your placemat and use it!

8 Repeat the entire process for as many place settings as you wish to have.

Tip:

I have listed basting spray as optional to layering and holding together this project and the three projects that follow. You can use safety pins instead, although the spray is extremely easy to use and works quite well. Just please, as with any spray, do not use near a bird.

Step 6

Flower Baskets Table Runner

A set table is not complete without a pretty table runner to pull the look all together. Here, using the same design as the placemats and the quilt, is yet another variation of the springtime Flower Basket design.

Finished Size

16" x 42" before washing

Materials

16" x 42" table runner foundation fabric

16" x 42" table runner backing fabric

16" x 42" batting

Scraps of fabric for bows, leaves, and three layers of the flowers

Quilting thread

Basting spray (optional)

Cutting Plan

Using the patterns on pages 28-29, cut six leaves, two bows, and all layers of the two flowers for two each.

Instructions

1 To make the point at each end of the table runner, make a mark or snip at the center of the end. Measure 8" up each side of the table runner and make a mark. Draw lines and cut along the lines. Do this for both the foundation and the backing.

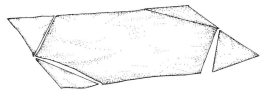

Step 1

2 Use the foundation or backing fabric as a pattern to make the point on the batting. Trim the entire piece of batting ½" all the way around.

3 Arrange the three layers of the table runner, starting with backing fabric right-side down, then center the batting on the wrong side of the backing, and place the foundation fabric right-side up on top of the batting, matching the raw edges with those of the backing fabric. Pin the layers together or use the basting spray as you layer.

4 Referring to the project layout, arrange the appliqués on the foundation fabric. Pin and stitch them ¼" in from the raw edges.

5 Stitch ½" from the raw edges all the way around the outside of the table runner.

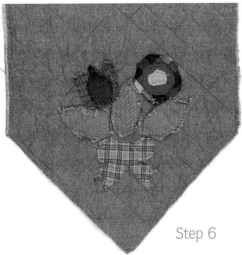

6 Quilt the table runner as shown at right, or in your own design.

7 Wash your table runner and use it

Step 6

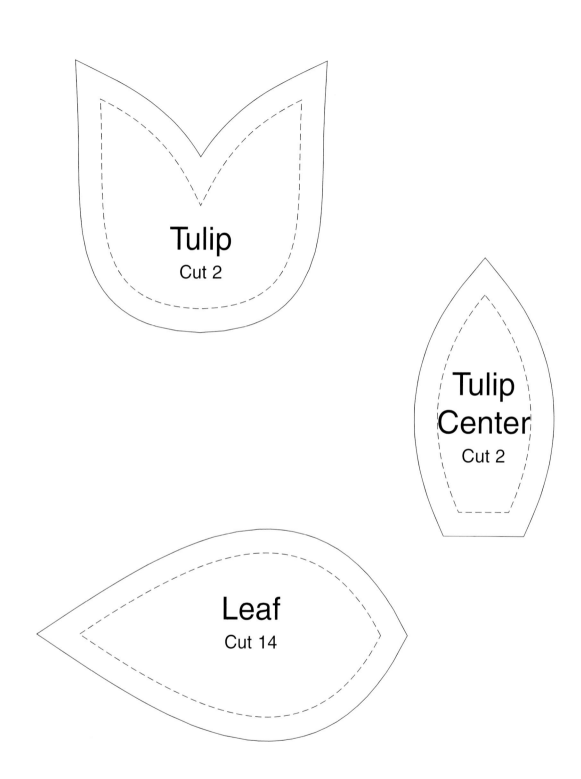

Tulip
Cut 2

Tulip
Center
Cut 2

Leaf
Cut 14

*Note: Numbers to be cut are totals for four placemats and the table runner combined.

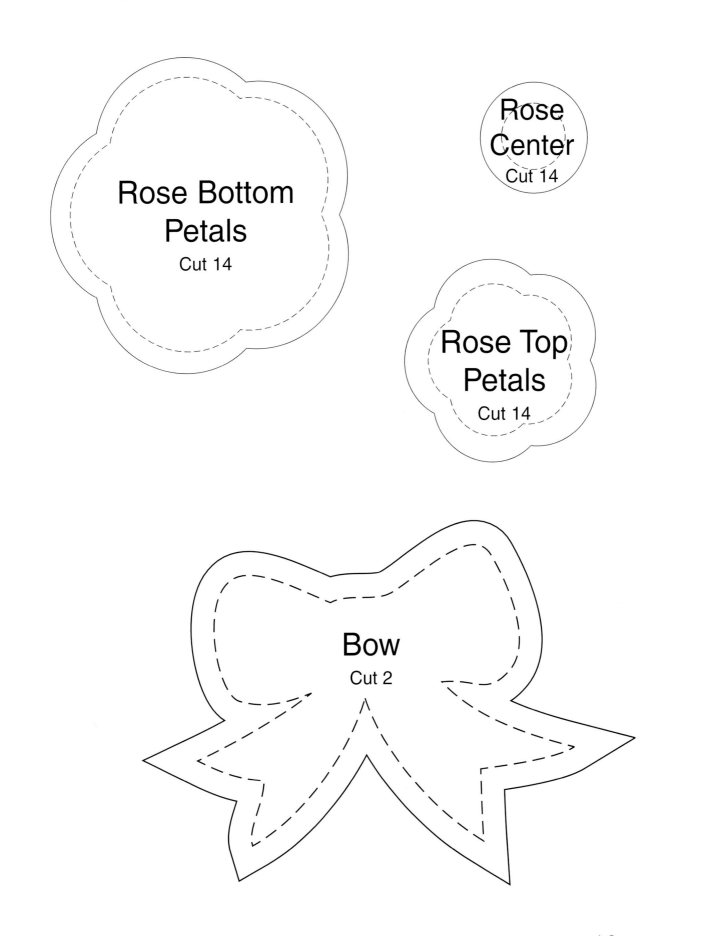

Rose Bottom
Petals

Cut 14

Rose
Center

Cut 14

Rose Top
Petals

Cut 14

Bow

Cut 2

Snowflake Placemats

The Flower Basket Placemats are
perfect for spring and summer, but when the
cold weather sets in, you'll want to adorn your table
with something more seasonally appropriate. These Snowflake
Placemats are sure to do the trick, adding warmth to your table
even when it's cold outside!

Finished Size

14" x 18" before washing

Materials

14" x 18" placemat foundation fabric
14" x 18" placemat backing fabric
13" x 17" batting
¼-yard white-on-white fabric for
   snowflakes

Quilting thread
Basting spray (optional)

Cutting Plan

Using five of the snowflake patterns on
   pages 34-35, cut five snowflakes
   from the white-on-white fabric.

Instructions

1. Arrange the three layers of the placemat, starting with backing fabric right-side down, then center the batting on the wrong side of the backing, and place the foundation fabric right-side up on top of the batting, matching the raw edges with those of the backing fabric. Pin the layers together or use the basting spray as you layer.

2. Referring to the placemat layout at right, arrange the snowflakes on the foundation fabric. Pin.

3. Using the quilting thread, stitch ¼" in from the raw edges of the snowflakes.

4. Stitch ½" from the raw edges all the way around the outside of the placemat.

5. Quilt the placemat as shown at right, which involves stitching inside each snowflake, following its design, and then sewing squiggles and stars in-between flakes. Or try your own design.

6. Wash your placemat and use it!

7. Repeat the entire process for as many place settings as you wish to have.

Step 2
Snowflake Placemat Layout

Step 5
Before washing (red)
and after (blue)

Snowflake Table Runner

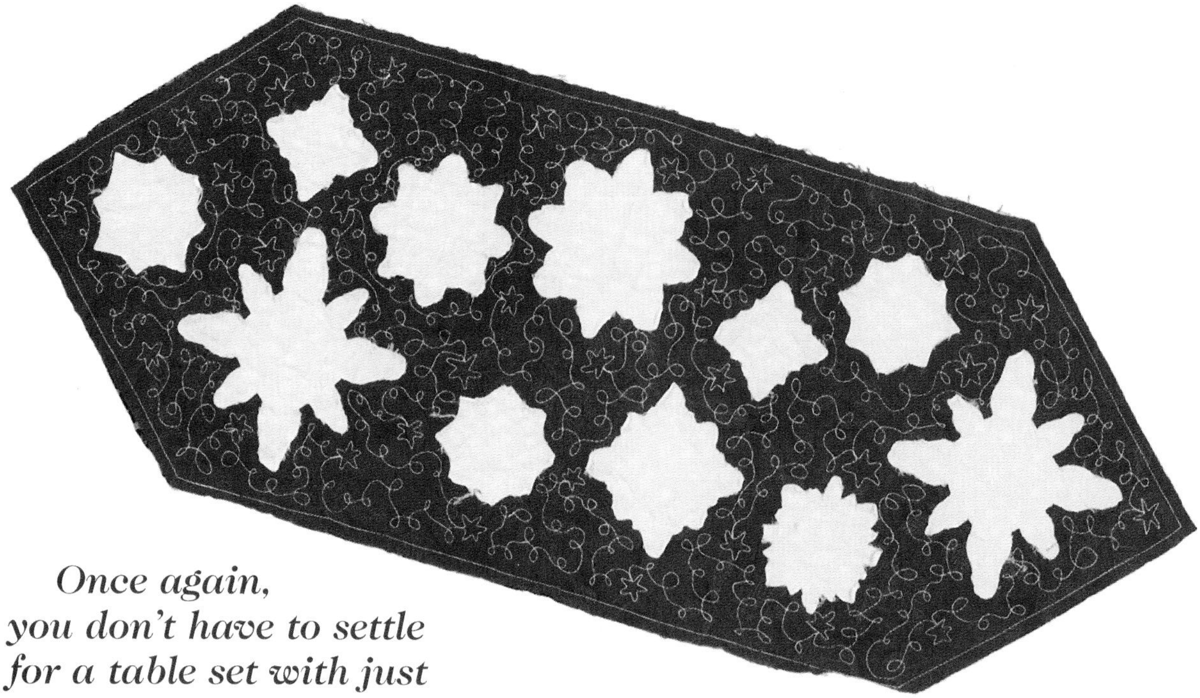

Once again,
you don't have to settle
for a table set with just
placemats. As with the Flower Basket
design, the Snowflake design is easily adapted to create a
pretty table runner.

Finished Size

16" x 42" before washing

Materials

16" x 42" table runner foundation
   fabric
16" x 42" table runner backing fabric
16" x 42" batting
¼-yard white-on-white fabric for
   snowflakes
Quilting thread
Basting spray (optional)

Cutting Plan

Using eleven of the snowflake patterns
   on pages 34-35, cut snowflakes
   from the white-on-white fabric.

Instructions

1 To make the point at each end of the table runner, make a mark or snip at the center of the end. Measure 8" up each side of the table runner and make a mark. Draw lines and cut along the lines. Do this for both the foundation and the backing.

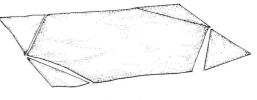

Step 1

2 Use the foundation or backing fabric as a pattern to make the point on the batting. Further trim the points ¼" so that the entire piece of batting is ½" all the way around smaller than the foundation and backing pieces.

3 Arrange the three layers of the table runner, starting with backing fabric right-side down, then center the batting on the wrong side of the backing, and place the foundation fabric right-side up on top of the batting, matching the raw edges with those of the backing fabric. Pin the layers together or use the basting spray as you layer.

4 Referring to the placemat layout at the top of this page, arrange the snowflakes on the foundation fabric. Pin and stitch them ¼" in from the raw edges of each piece.

5 Stitch ½" from the raw edges all the way around the outside of the table runner.

6 Quilt the table runner as shown at right (same as for the placemats), or in your own design.

Step 6

7 Wash your table runner and use it!

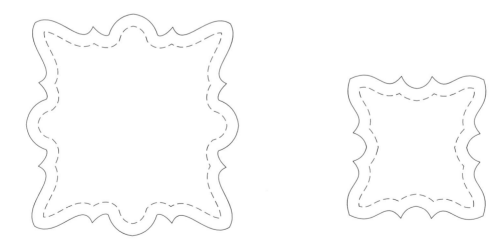

Enlarge 200%

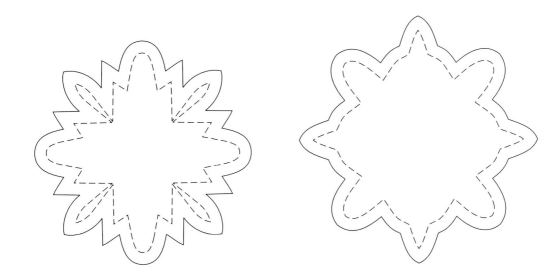

Enlarge 200%

Tisket Tasket KittyBaskets and Dressed to Bark

The inspiration for the kitty quilt comes from my laundry basket. You see, I have three kitties any of which at one time or another can be found snoozing in the laundry basket—wherever it may be. Currently ten-week-old Miss Lora Brody (of bread-making fame) is purring away in what appears to be the throne of choice for kitties.

When the vision of this quilt hit, I hurriedly sketched it down and then close on its heels (paws?), another design came in the form of dressed dogs.

I dedicate these quilts to Savannah and Ben Loomis, kindred souls in kitty/doggie love.

If you choose to use a border print for your quilt as I did for my kitty quilt, the width of the print on the border fabric chosen will determine the width to cut the borders. It doesn't matter what size you cut your borders, just center the fabric motif on the strip. If the borders end up wider than mine, do remember to cut your batting and backing larger accordingly.

Finished Size

31" x 48" before washing

Block Size

10" x 12"

Materials

¾-yard block background fabric

¼-yard yellow print for sashing the blocks

¼-yard red inner border fabric

1½ yards border print fabric for outside border

1½ yards backing fabric

40" x 58" piece of batting

½-yard binding fabric

Cutting Plan

Cut six 10½" x 12½" block background squares.

Cut the sashing fabric into 1½" strips.

Cut the red inner border fabric into three 1" strips.

Cut the border fabric into four 4"-wide strips along the length of the fabric.

Cut the appliqué pieces according to the instructions on the patterns, pages 41-45.

Cut five 2½" strips for binding.

Step 1
Kitties Layout Diagram

Instructions:

1 Refer to the quilt layout diagrams (at left on this page and in the upper right on the next page) to appliqué the blocks.

For Kitties:

a. Position the basket pieces in the centers of the background squares. Stitch around the raw edges, a generous ⅛" from the edge.

b. Place the bow, kitty head, and paws in position. Appliqué in place.

c. Position the leaves and appliqué.

d. Place the red flower, appliqué, and place the yellow center and appliqué.

e. Embroider the faces by hand or machine.

For Doggies:

a. Lay out each block, and then remove pieces to sew down the bottom-most layer, usually the tail. To help you determine placement, the bottoms of my dogs are about 2½" above the bottom edge of the square.

b. Embroider the faces by hand or machine.

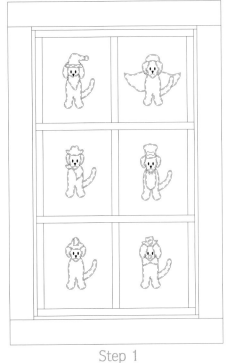

Step 1
Doggies Layout Diagram

2 Stitch sashing strips to the left sides of each block. Stitch sashing strips to the right sides of three of the blocks. Press the seam allowances toward the sashing strips.

3 Stitch the blocks together into pairs.

4 Stitch sashing strips to the tops of the three sets of blocks.

5 Stitch sashing strips to the bottom on one set of blocks. Stitch the sets together. Press the seam allowances toward the sashing strips.

6 Stitch a red inner border strip to each side of the blocks. Trim. Press the seam allowances toward the blocks.

Step 3

Step 4

Step 5

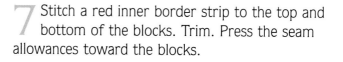

Step 7

Step 8

7 Stitch a red inner border strip to the top and bottom of the blocks. Trim. Press the seam allowances toward the blocks.

8 To apply mitered borders, refer to page 13.

9 Follow the instructions for preparing for quilting on page 14 and quilt as shown in the close-up photos below, or in your own design.

10 Follow the instructions on pages 16-17 to bind your quilt.

Step 9

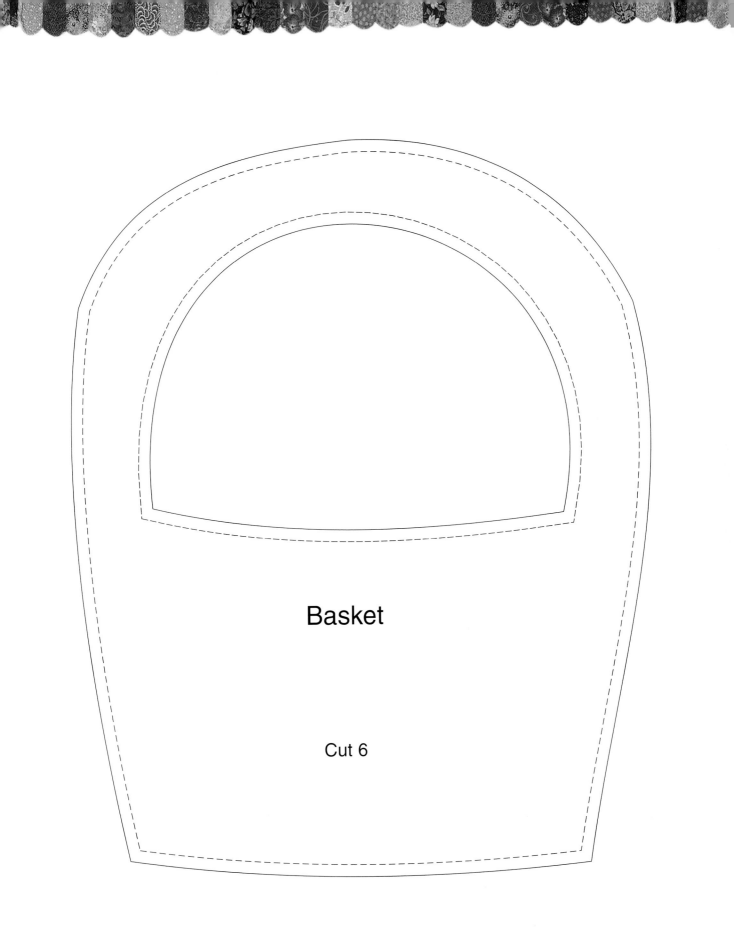

Basket

Cut 6

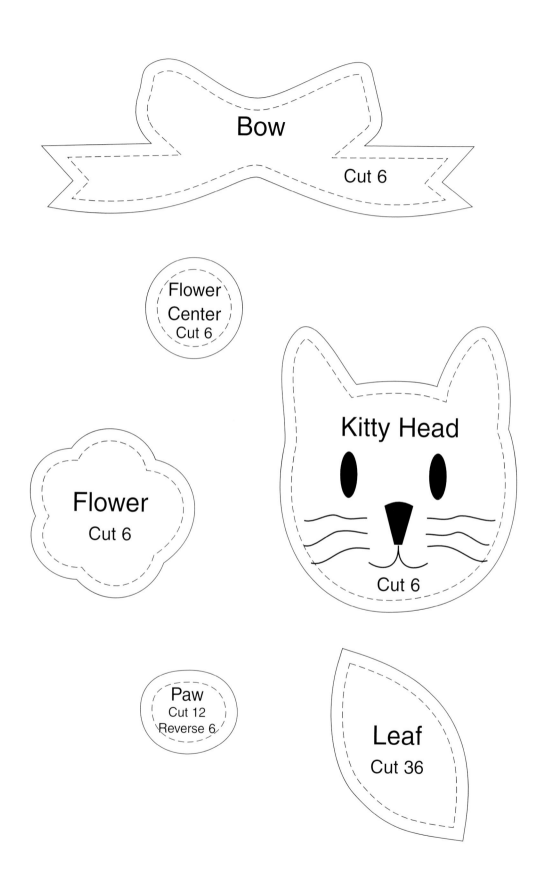

Bow

Cut 6

Flower
Center
Cut 6

Kitty Head

Cut 6

Flower
Cut 6

Paw
Cut 12
Reverse 6

Leaf
Cut 36

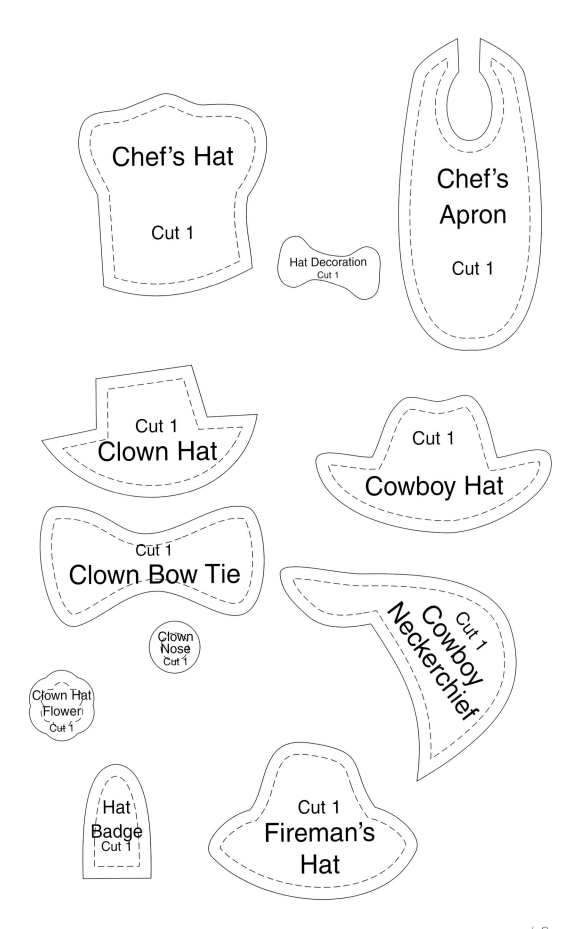

Chef's Hat
Cut 1

Hat Decoration
Cut 1

Chef's Apron
Cut 1

Cut 1
Clown Hat

Cut 1
Cowboy Hat

Cut 1
Clown Bow Tie

Clown Nose
Cut 1

Cut 1
Cowboy Neckerchief

Clown Hat Flower
Cut 1

Hat Badge
Cut 1

Cut 1
Fireman's Hat

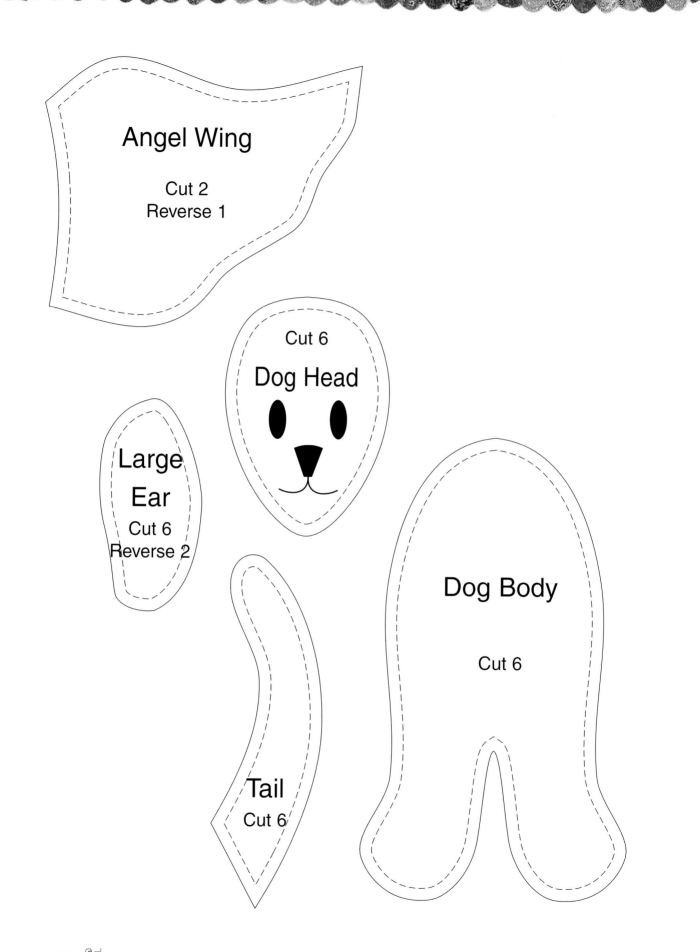

Angel Wing

Cut 2
Reverse 1

Dog Head

Cut 6

Large
Ear

Cut 6
Reverse 2

Dog Body

Cut 6

Tail

Cut 6

Small
Ear

Cut 6
Reverse 2

Santa Hat
Pom Pom
Cut 1

Halo

Cut 1

Santa Hat Trim   Cut 1

Santa Hat

Cut 1

Santa
Beard

Cut 1

Climbing Rose Log Cabin

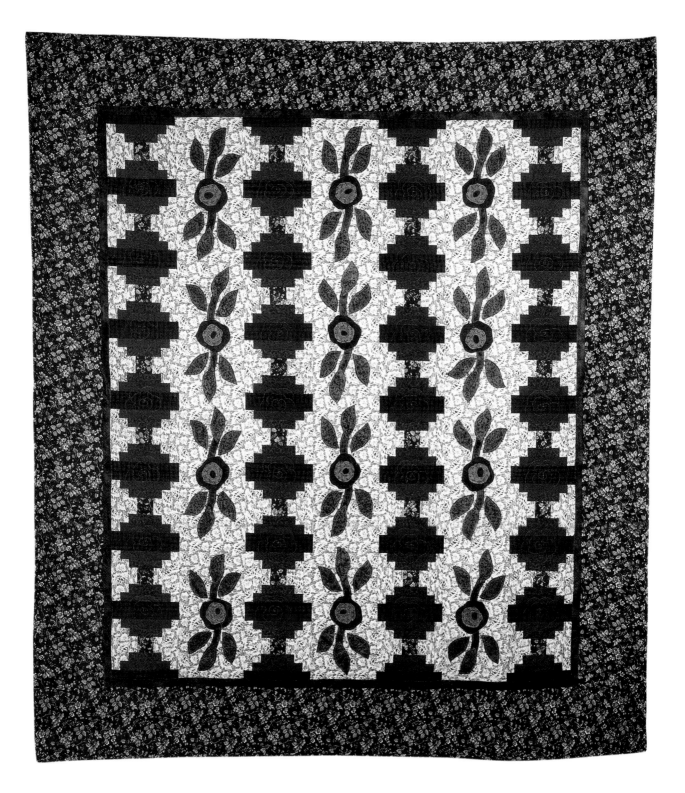

Alternate strips of paper-pieced log cabin blocks set in Courthouse Steps fashion form a trellis for the strips of raw-edge appliquéd rose vines to climb on this twin-size quilt.

The top is constructed in the traditional manner, and quilted as a completed top. Mine was long-arm quilted with a rose pattern (see Sources, page 95) to complement the theme of the quilt.

Finished Size

74" x 82" before washing

Block Size

8"

Materials

3 yards beige/red background fabric

¾-yard green border fabric

2 yards large flowered print fabric for border

¾-yard dark red large print fabric for log 1

½-yard dark red print fabric for logs 4 and 5

1 yard dark red print fabric for logs 8 and 9

1¼ yards dark red print fabric for logs 12 and 13

½-yard green print fabric for leaves and stems

¼-yard dark red fabric for rose layer 1

⅛-yard pink fabric for rose layer 2

Scrap of dark red fabric for rose layer 3

84" x 90" batting

Backing

Cutting Plan

Cut three strips of background fabric 8½" x 64½" for setting between the log cabin block strips.

Cut the green fabric into eight 1½"-wide strips.

Cut the border fabric into eight 8½"-wide pieces.

Cut the log 1 fabrics into 3" strips.

Cut the remaining log fabrics into 2" strips.

Shown from bottom side. This side will have been down when you stitch.

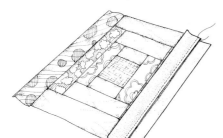

Step 5

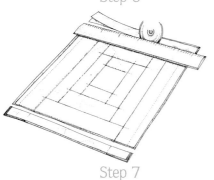

Step 6

Step 7

Tip:

Leave the paper foundation in place until the quilt top is completed. Blocks are easier to align this way and will not become distorted by the tearing process. Also, do not worry about the grain line of the block edges. The paper foundation stabilizes the edges throughout the construction process.

Instructions

Paper-Piecing the Log Cabin Blocks

1 Copy the patterns for the log cabin blocks, pages 52-53, onto paper. Transfer all markings.

2 Set your machine to a stitch length of eighteen to twenty stitches per inch. The short stitch length creates a stronger stitch that won't come apart when tearing the paper away, and the closely spaced perforations also facilitate the tearing away of the paper.

3 Cut a piece of fabric for log 1 at least ½" larger than the area on the paper that it will cover. Place log 1 on the unmarked side of the foundation with the wrong side facing the paper. If you wish, use a small dab of fabric glue stick to hold the fabric to the paper.

4 With right sides together, place log 2 against log 1 so that the majority of log 2 is over area 1. Leave nearly ½" of fabric extending into the area marked 2. Working from the marked side of the foundation, stitch along the seam line between areas 1 and 2. Begin and end the stitching several stitches beyond the ends of the line.

5 Flip up log 2 to be sure it covers the area marked 2 in the pattern when it is pressed into place. Trim the seam allowance to ¼". Fold log 2 over the seam and press it in place.

6 Add the remaining pieces in numerical order in the same manner.

7 Lay the block, fabric side down (marked paper foundation up), on a cutting mat. Using a rotary cutter and ruler, trim the edges of the block piece along the dashed lines. This leaves a ¼" seam allowance around the block. Make sure you cut through the paper foundation and fabric.

Rose Vine Appliqué

8 Copy the patterns for the appliqué pieces, as instructed on page 51. Place the large background sections on your work surface.

9 Consulting the photo of the finished quilt on page 46, arrange the vines, roses, and leaves, and pin to the background sections.

10 Starting with the vine stems, then the roses, and lastly the leaves, appliqué them to the quilt top by machine-stitching ⅛" from the raw edge. For the roses, sew the bottom larger piece of the rose first, then add each layer in turn, working up to the smallest section.

Construction

11 Arrange the log cabin blocks into four sets of eight blocks each with the dark red fabrics adjoining. Stitch each strip together.

12 Arrange the strips of blocks and the appliquéd sections as they will appear on the finished quilt top. Sew them together.

13 Stitch the eight green inner border strips into two sets of two each. Press the seams to one side.

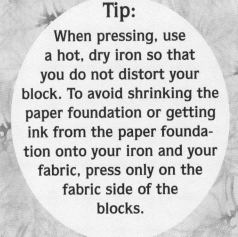

Tip:
When pressing, use a hot, dry iron so that you do not distort your block. To avoid shrinking the paper foundation or getting ink from the paper foundation onto your iron and your fabric, press only on the fabric side of the blocks.

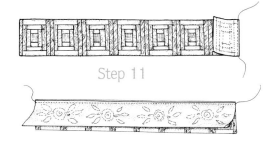

Step 11

Step 12

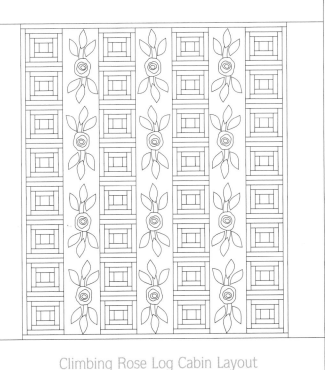

Climbing Rose Log Cabin Layout

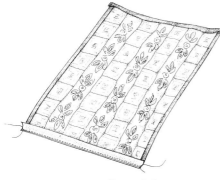

Step 14

Step 16

14 Stitch one set of strips to each side of the quilt top. Trim. Press the seam allowances toward the strips. Repeat for the top and bottom edges of the quilt top.

15 Stitch the border pieces into two sets of two each. Press the seams to one side. Trim two sets to measure 66½" long.

16 Stitch to each side of the quilt top. Trim. Press the seam allowances toward the strips. Repeat for the top and bottom edges of the quilt top, cutting the paired sets to 82½" long.

17 Remove the paper from the paper-pieced blocks.

18 Follow the instructions on page 14 to layer and sandwich your quilt.

19 Quilt as shown at right, or in your own design.

20 Bind your quilt as instructed on pages 16-17.

Step 19

Tip:

Glenda used the Rose Vine pattern to quilt this quilt. She used just the rose portion on the dark red sections of the log cabin blocks, quilted a free-form loop in the background fabric of the appliqué sections, and used the trellis pattern in the borders. To obtain the patterns, see the Sources section on page 95.

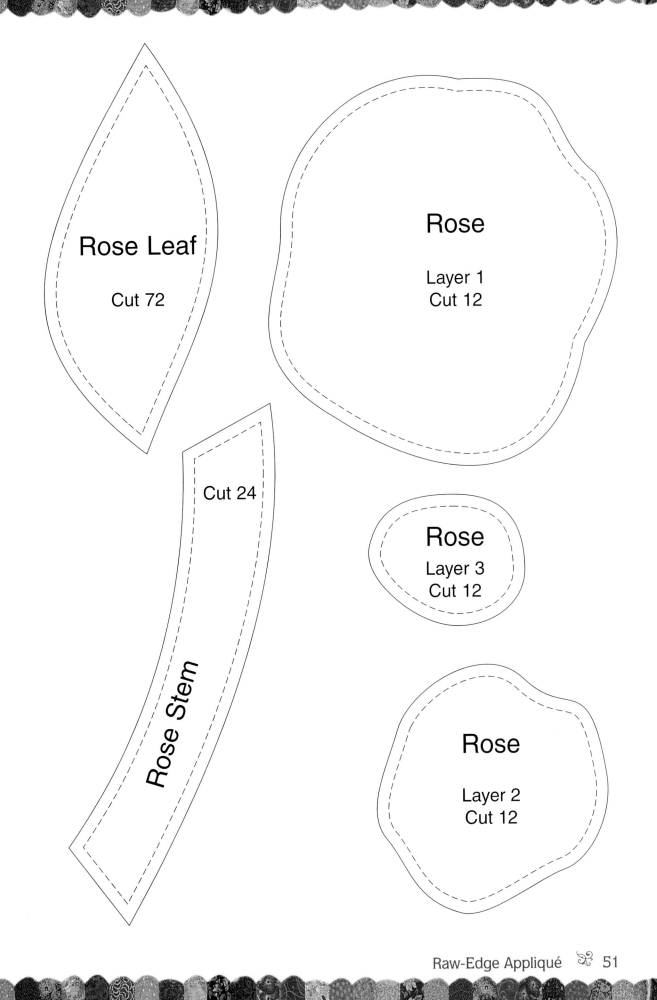

Rose Leaf

Cut 72

Rose

Layer 1
Cut 12

Cut 24

Rose

Layer 3
Cut 12

Rose Stem

Rose

Layer 2
Cut 12

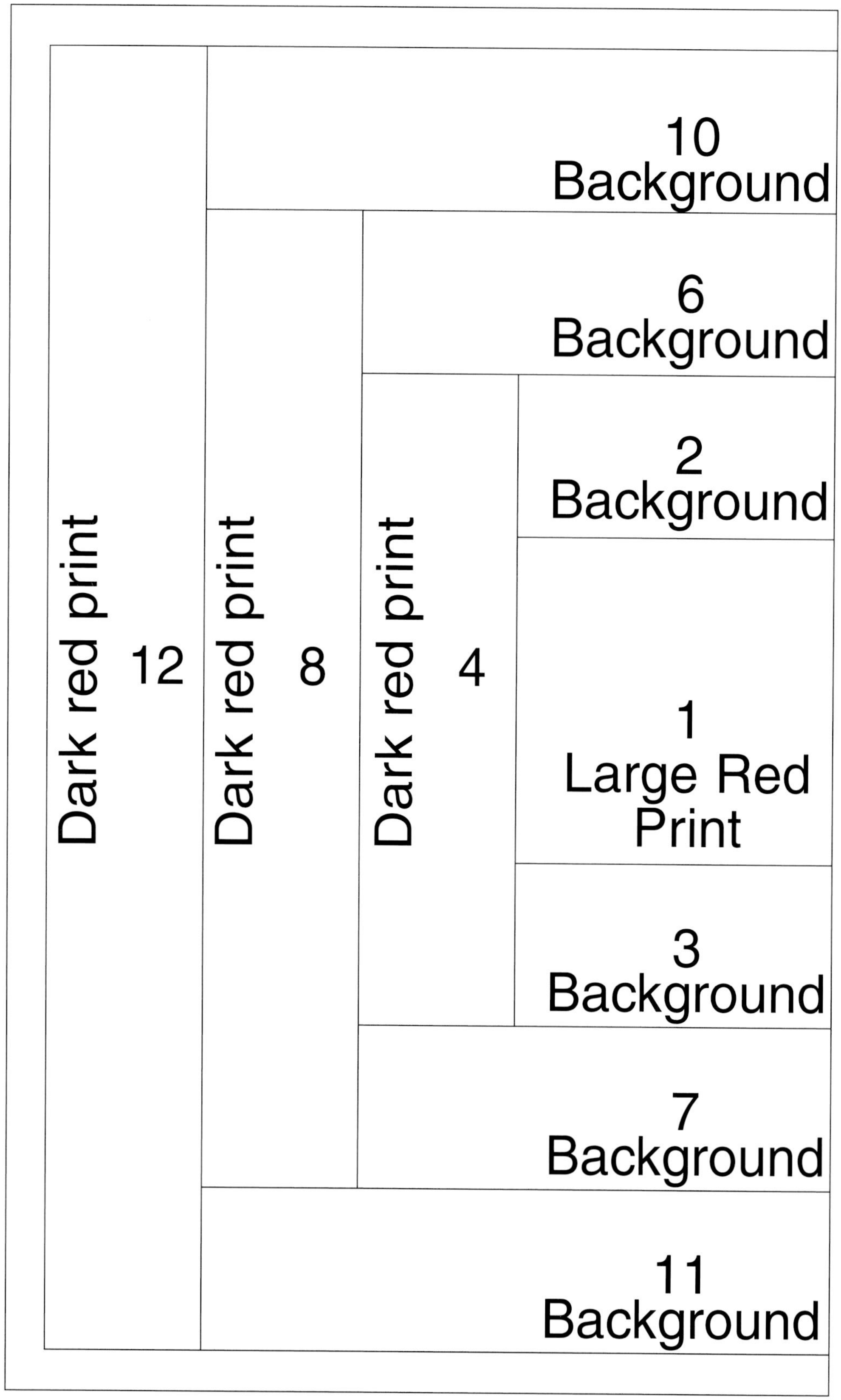
10
Background
6
Background
2
Background
1
Large Red
Print
3
Background
7
Background
11
Background
Dark red print
12
Dark red print
8
Dark red print
4

Rose Log Cabin Block Part 1: Butt and tape here to Part 2

Rose Log Cabin Block Part 2: Butt and tape here to Part 1

Dark red print 13

Dark red print 9

Dark red print 5

Dresden Plate

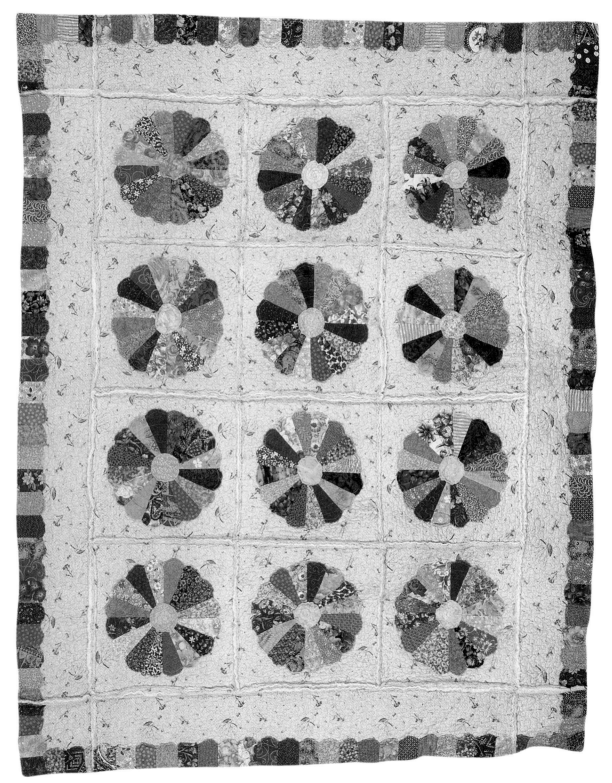

A toasty warm version of a treasured classic pattern, the raw-edge appliqué Dresden Plate conjures up visions of a comfy chair, a pot of tea, a kitty for the lap, and a good book.

Raw-edge appliqué makes the sewing of the plates easy, and the frayed edges add to the charm of the design.

Each block and border section is appliquéd and quilted, then sewn together with seam allowances to the front. Note that since I was using a natural-colored fabric for my block background and a natural batting, I cut the batting the same size as I did my blocks. The batting therefore shows in the exposed seams where the blocks are joined.

If you'd rather not see the batting on your finished quilts, reduce the size you cut the batting sections by ½" in each direction.

Finished Size

56" x 70" before washing

Block Size

14"

Materials (42"-wide fabric)

3 yards total assorted print fabrics for
    Dresden blades
Scraps of yellow for plate centers
2½ yards beige background fabric
2½ yards backing
2½ yards batting or a single-bed-size
    batt

Cutting Plan

Using the Dresden Plate Blade pattern
    on page 59, cut sixteen "blades"
    for each of the twelve Dresden
    Plate blocks.
Cut 128 3" squares from the assorted
    blade fabrics for the border edge.
Using the Dresden Plate Center
    pattern, cut twelve yellow plate
    circles from the yellow fabric
    scraps.
Cut each of the background, batting,
    and backing fabrics in turn into:
    Twelve 14½" squares
    Two 7½" x 56½" side border
    sections
    Two 7½" x 42½" top and bottom
    border sections
    Four 7½" square corner border
    sections

Instructions

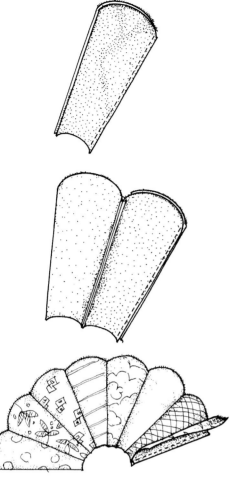

1 Right sides facing, stitch two "blades" together along one edge.

   Add six more "blades" to make a set of eight. Repeat to make two sets.

2 Press the seam allowances in one direction.

3 Lay out the half sets and pair them up. Stitch the halves together.

4 Fold the background squares in half and press gently. Unfold. Fold in half again and press gently. Unfold. This gives you placement markings.

5 Position a Dresden Plate on a background square, using the pressed markings as centering guides. Pin in place.

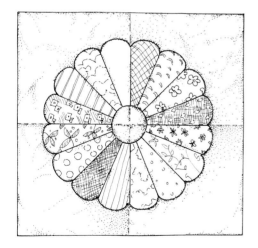

Step 1

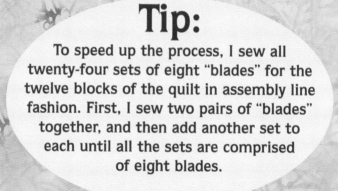

Tip:

To speed up the process, I sew all twenty-four sets of eight "blades" for the twelve blocks of the quilt in assembly line fashion. First, I sew two pairs of "blades" together, and then add another set to each until all the sets are comprised of eight blades.

Step 5

6 Lay a yellow Dresden Plate center in place. Pin.

7 Stitch ¼" from the raw edges of the plate center and from the outer edges of the fan blades.

Repeat steps 1 through 7 to make twelve blocks.

8 Layer the backing, batting, and quilt top pieces for the blocks and all of the border sections as instructed on page 14.

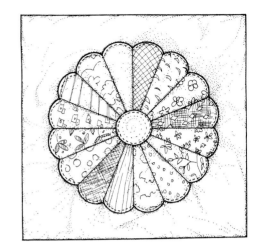

Step 7

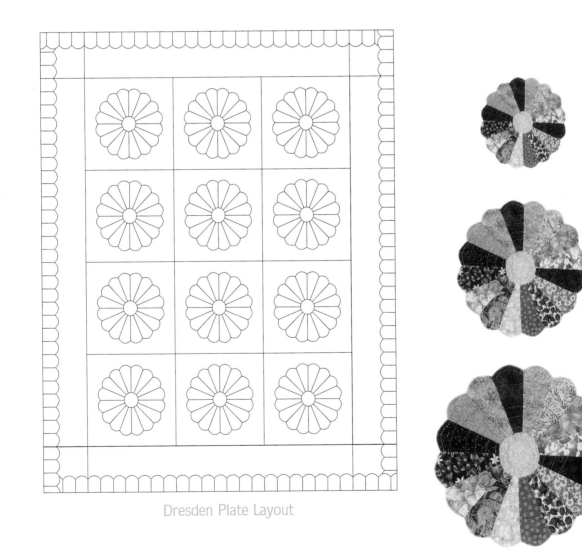

Dresden Plate Layout

Step 9

9 Quilt each section up to ¼" from the raw edges. As shown in the close-up photo above, I quilted my Dresden Plates using a spiral starting from the center out, and I meandered in the background.

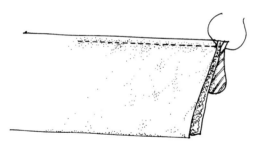

10 Right sides facing, stitch the 3" border edging squares together randomly. Make two sections of twenty-eight squares each for the sides of the quilt and twenty-one for the top and bottom. Make four sets each of four and three squares for the corners. Press the seam allowances to one side.

Using the Dresden Plate Blade pattern, cut the raw edges of one edge of the row of squares into curves.

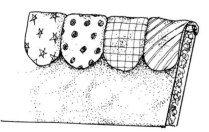

Step 11

11 Right sides facing, stitch the strips to the back of the quilt, using a ¼" seam allowance. For the corners, sew the three-square pieces to one corner and then overlap with the four-square section as shown. Fold to the front. Press.

Stitch ¼" from the raw edges of the curved blade of the border edge strips and ¼" from the outside edge of each border section.

12 Backing sides facing, stitch the blocks together, first making four rows of three blocks each, and then sewing the rows together. Use a ¼" seam allowance.

Add the side borders. Sew the corner borders to the ends of the top and bottom borders. Sew the top and bottom borders to the quilt.

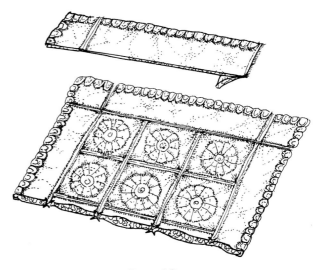

Step 12

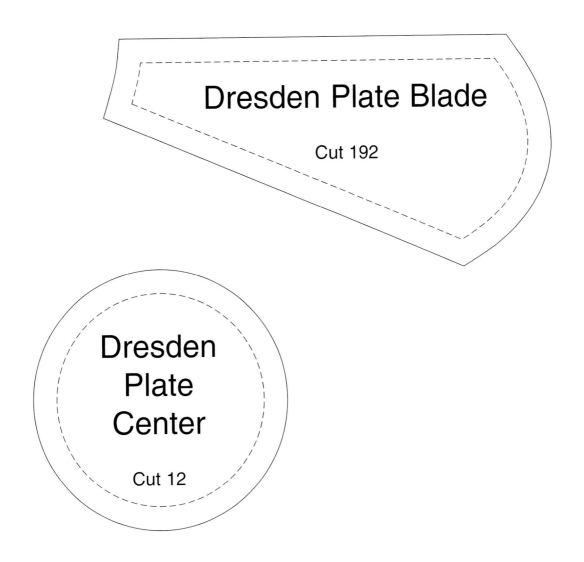

Dresden Plate Blade

Cut 192

Dresden Plate Center

Cut 12

Frayed Log Cabin

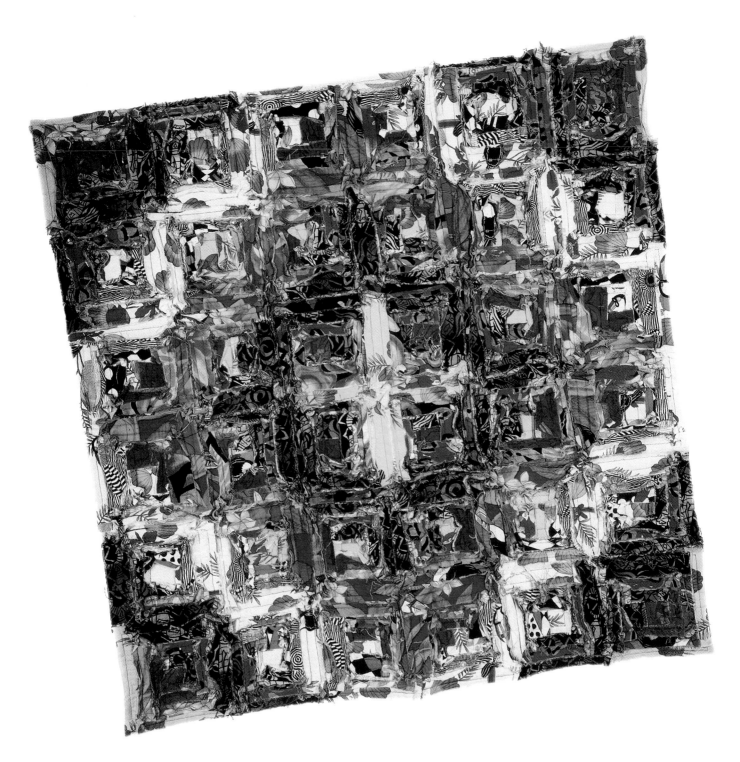

A contemporary interpretation of an old favorite, this whole cloth Log Cabin proudly displays its seam allowances as an intrinsic part of the design.

The project is constructed in quilt-as-you-go style. First, a background fabric is marked with the log cabin blocks. Next, the background is layered with the backing and batting. Then, the print fabric strips, or logs, are machine-sewn to the quilt sandwich. The logs are ½" larger all around than the sections they are sewn to, resulting in a ½" seam allowance that is free to fray on the quilt surface.

I chose loud tropical conversational prints for this quilt in three color families: yellow and red/orange fabrics with a good sprinkling of green in the prints; purple and blue fabrics with some black and the reds and greens in them; and white fabrics with black and greens, blues, purples, and yellows. Pay no concern as to whether the fabrics match. Choose them for color and for a variety of scales and types of prints. You won't see the fabrics in the finished quilt, just the texture and color they provide.

Finished Size

48" square before washing

Block Size

8"

Materials

2 yards assorted yellow and
    red fabrics
2 yards assorted blue and
    purple fabrics
1½ yards assorted white fabrics
3 yards background fabric
3 yards backing fabric
Batting
Thread

Cutting Plan

Cut three 3" strips of yellow log fabric and cut into twenty-eight 3" squares for the
    center, No. 1 center pieces, of the yellow/blue and white/yellow blocks.
Cut one 3" strip of white log fabric into eight 3" squares for the No. 1 center
    pieces of the blue/white blocks.
Cut the remaining "log" fabrics into strips for pieces No. 2 through No. 13 accord-
    ing to the chart below. You can cut them all at once and label the stacks, or
    keep a rotary cutter and mat by your sewing machine and cut them as you go.

Piece	Cut Size	Fabric Color Family		
		16 Yellow/Blue Blocks	8 Blue/White Blocks	12 White/Yellow Blocks
1	3" x 3"	yellow	white	yellow
2	2" x 3"	yellow	white	yellow
3	2" x 4"	yellow	white	yellow
4	2" x 4"	blue	blue	white
5	2" x 5"	blue	blue	white
6	2" x 5"	yellow	white	yellow
7	2" x 6"	yellow	white	yellow
8	2" x 6"	blue	blue	white
9	2" x 7"	blue	blue	white
10	2" x 7"	yellow	white	yellow
11	2" x 8"	yellow	white	yellow
12	2" x 8"	blue	blue	white
13	2" x 9"	blue	blue	white

Instructions

1 Cut the background fabric into two 1½-yard pieces. Trim away selvedge edges and seam the two pieces together along one set of these selvedge edges to form one big rectangle. Repeat for the backing fabric. Press the seams to one side.

2 To find the center of the background fabric, fold the fabric in half and in half again. Press the folds. Open up. To provide placement lines for marking the log cabin squares, make a grid of 8" squares starting at the center and using the folds as placement lines.

3 Copy the log cabin block pattern, pages 66-67. Using a light box, trace the pattern into each of the 8" squares you marked on the background fabric. Working from the center out, place the block pattern with the arrow pointing as shown in the quilt layout, lower right corner of this page.

Following the chart below, mark each block or log with color placement information.

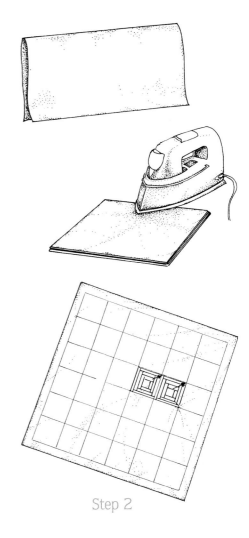

Step 2

Fabric Color Family Block Layout

Yellow/Blue Block

Blue/White Block

White/Yellow Block

Step 3
Frayed Log Cabin Layout

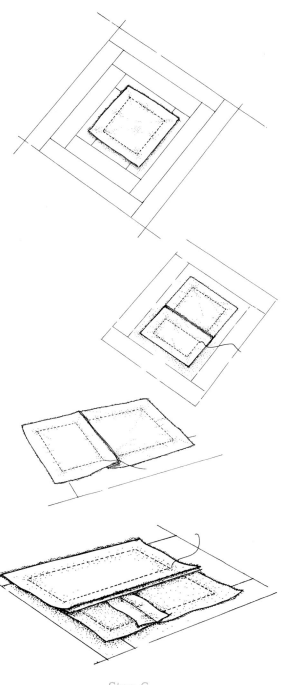

Step 6

4 Make a quilt sandwich as described on page 14.

5 Thread-baste the layers together. Don't use safety pins or you'll be breaking needles as you sew!

6 Starting with one of the four log cabin squares at the center of the quilt, sew the "logs" in place. The ½" seam allowances of each "log" will extend past the marked line by ½".

Sew piece 1 in place, overlapping the stitching where you begin and end sewing the square, and appliquéing and quilting at the same time by sewing through the entire quilt sandwich.

Fold back the edge of log 1 adjoining section 2 and sew log 2 in place. Continue on adding logs in the numerical sequence. Complete all of the squares this way.

Tip:
If you do not have access to a light box, place a lamp under a glass table, or if you have a Sew Steady clear acrylic table (see Sources) such as the one I bought for my Bernina, shine a light under it for a handy light box.

7 Clip all thread ends. Trim batting and backing to ¼" beyond the last stitching. Trim yellow background fabric to 1½" from the outermost stitching from the appliquéd log cabin blocks. Fold the yellow background fabric to the back of the quilt, turning under a ¼" seam allowance and slip stitching to the back of the quilt.

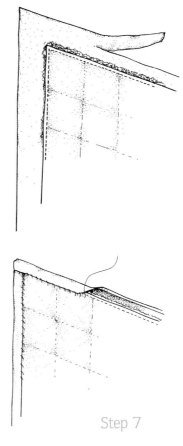

Step 7

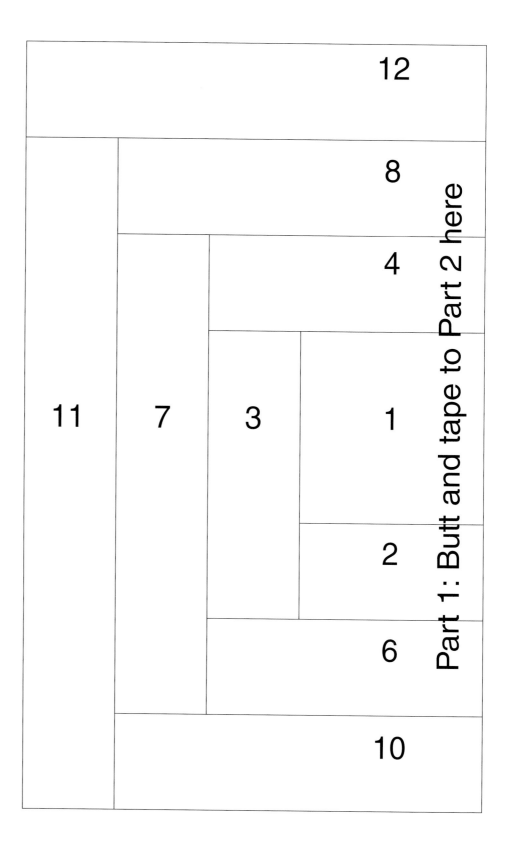

Part 1: Butt and tape to Part 2 here

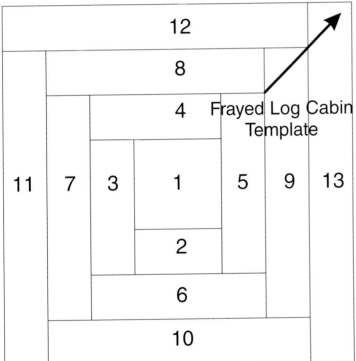

12

8

4   Frayed Log Cabin
Template

11 | 7 | 3 | 1 | 5 | 9 | 13

2

6

10

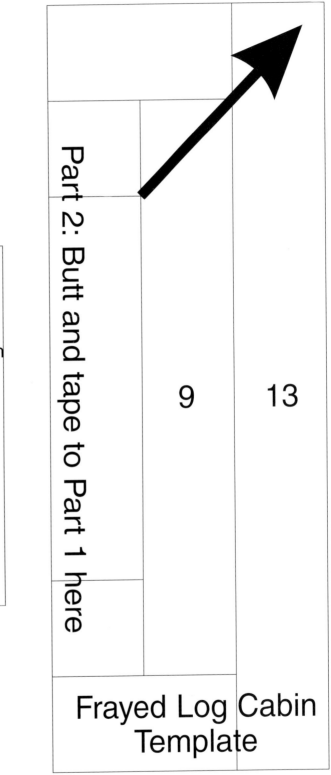

Part 2: Butt and tape to Part 1 here

9   13

Frayed Log Cabin
Template

Boston Uncommon

Traditionally a quilt of squares sewn together and set on point, the Raw-Edge Appliqué version of Boston Common is anything but conventional. The squares are first stitched down leaving ½" seam allowances free, and the quilt is quilted with a fun variegated thread. The striped fabric used for the border calls for mitered corners. If you haven't tackled mitered corners before, try my instructions on page 13. They're easier than you think!

Finished Size

46" x 59½" before washing

Materials

1¾ yards background fabric
¼-yard pink 1 fabric
⅓-yard green 1
½-yard purple
⅝-yard green 2
¾-yard pink 2
1 yard green 3
1¼ yards striped fabric for border
3 yards backing fabric
54" x 68" batting
½-yard binding fabric
Colored sewing thread (I used fuchsia)
Quilting thread (I used purple Colours by YLI. See Sources.)

Cutting Plan

From the background fabric, cut a rectangle 35½" x 49½".
From the border fabric, cut eight strips 5¾" wide and the width of the fabric.
Cut 4½" squares as follows:
  Five pink 1
  Sixteen green 1
  Twenty-four purple
  Thirty-two green 2
  Forty pink 2
  Forty-eight green 3
Backing 54" x 68"
Cut seven 2½"-wide strips for binding.

Step 1
Boston Uncommon Layout

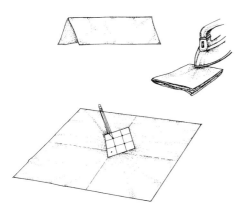

Step 1

Instructions

1 To find and mark the center of the background fabric, fold in half and in half again. Press the folds. Open up the fabric.

Referencing the quilt layout above, use the placement template on page 73 and a pencil or blue washout pen to mark the quilt top. Start at the center and work out, using the pressed folds and preceding dots as guides.

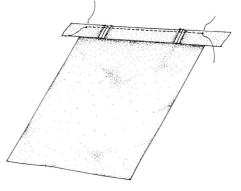

2 Cut two border strips into two pieces. Stitch
each of the two pieces to the ends of two other
border strips. Use these for the short edges of the
quilts. Stitch the remaining four strips into two sets
of two. These are for the long edges of the quilt.
Press the seam allowances to one side.

3 Center one border strip to one edge of the
background. Starting and stopping ¼" from the
edge of the background piece stitch, backstitching
at both ends of the seam. Repeat for the three
remaining border strips.

4 Following the instructions on page 13, miter
the border corners.

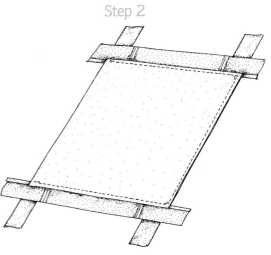

Step 3

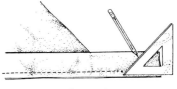

Step 4

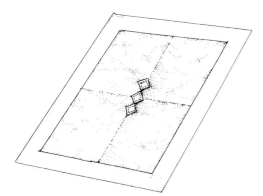

5 Starting with the pink squares at the center of the quilt, stitch the squares to the quilt top, using the marked dots for placement. The dots correspond to the intersections of the stitching lines, and will occur ½" inside the corners of the squares. Place the squares one at a time and, using a regular machine stitch, stitch ½" in from the raw edge of the square, overlapping the stitching to secure. Fold the seam allowances of the preceding squares back and out of the way as you add new ones.

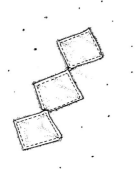

6 Repeat with all of the squares to complete the top. Note that the last row of squares will overlap onto the border, being centered over the seam.

7 Cut the backing fabric into two 1½-yard pieces. Trim selvedges and seam the two pieces together along one set of selvedge edges, right sides facing. Press the seam allowances to one side.

Step 5

8 Following the instructions on page 14, layer and baste your quilt sandwich together.

9 To quilt your quilt, stitch free-form flowers in each appliquéd square, and stitch in a wobbly line from quilt edge to quilt edge through the centers of the yellow background squares.

10 Bind your quilt as instructed on pages 16-17.

Step 9

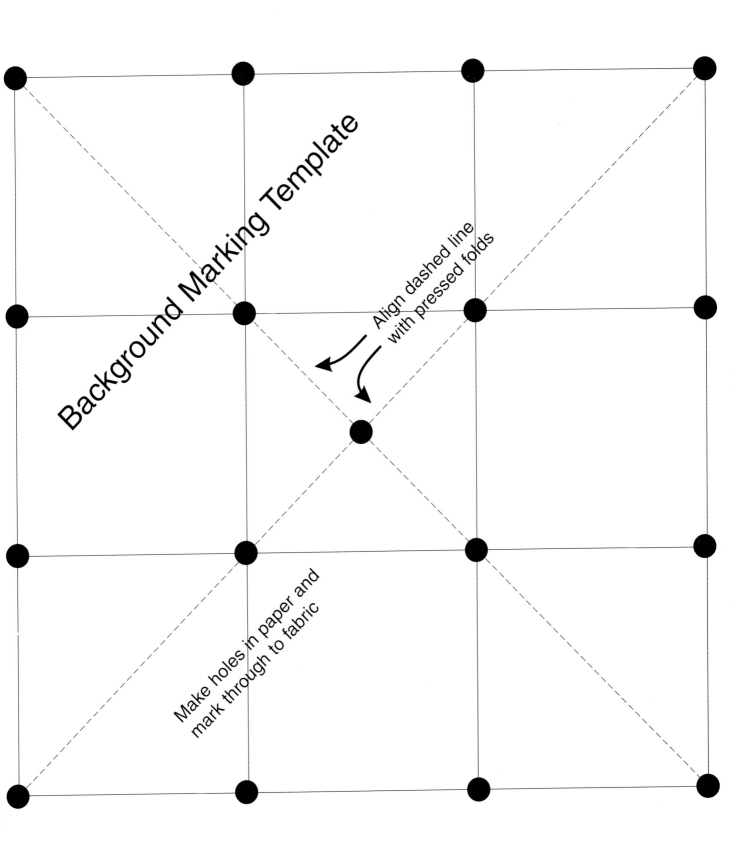

Background Marking Template

Align dashed line with pressed folds

Make holes in paper and mark through to fabric

American Lone Star

This gently patriotic quilt turns out to be apropos as I finish it here at the end of September 2001.

An extremely easy version of a quilt I've made using traditional methods, this one covers sewing faux paus with those sewing- and user-friendly frayed seam allowances.

Finished Size

40" square before washing

Materials

¾-yard total of assorted yellow print fabrics

⅓-yard total of assorted red print fabrics

½-yard total of assorted blue print fabrics

1 yard background fabric

1 yard border fabric

1½ yards backing fabric

Cutting Plan

Cut the background fabric 26½" square.

Using template on page 79, cut diamonds as follows:
   Fifty-six yellow
   Sixteen red
   Twenty-four blue

Cut four border pieces 7½" x 26½".

Cut four corner border pieces 7½" square.

Cut one backing square 26½".

Cut four border backing pieces 7½" x 26½".

Cut four border corner backing pieces 7½" square.

Cut one batting square 26½".

Cut four border batting pieces 7½" x 26½".

Cut four border corner batting pieces 7½" square.

Instructions

1 To find and mark the center of the background fabric, fold in half and in half again. Press the folds. Starting at the center, use the Diamond Marking Template on page 79 to mark the top.

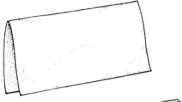

Step 1

2 Starting at the center with the yellow, raw-edge appliqué the star diamond pieces to the quilt top. Working out, appliqué the red and then the blue star diamonds. Use a ½" seam allowance.

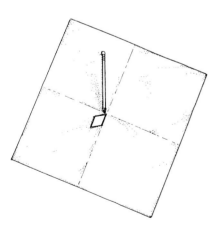

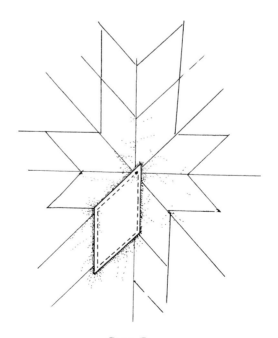

Step 2

Step 3
American Lone Star Layout

3 Referring to the quilt layout above, mark the border and border corner sections using the Diamond Marking Template, page 79.

4 Raw-edge appliqué the diamonds in place.

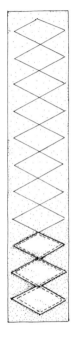

5 Layer and quilt the center section and the border sections, including the corners, as instructed on page 14.

Step 5

Step 4

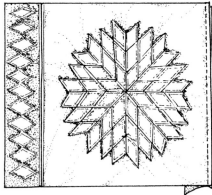

Step 6

6 With backing fabrics facing, stitch two border sections to opposite sides of the quilt center.

7 Again with backing fabrics facing, stitch the border corner sections to the ends of the two remaining border sections. Stitch to the remaining edges of the quilt top. Stitch ½" from the outer edges of the quilt, stopping and restarting at seams.

Step 7

Lone Star
Diamond Marking Template

Lone Star
Diamond Cutting Template

Drunkard's Path

Would you believe that this quilt is made from just two fabrics? The background is a black marbled fabric, and the raw-edge appliquéd print "path" pieces are cut from Monet-influenced landscape fabric. I cut my path pieces from the large areas of each color and then grouped and sewed the like colors to each of my blocks.

The amount of print landscape fabric you will need will be determined by the fabric you choose. For instance, if there is a lot of green and not as much of the blues, purples, and other colors, you may need more yardage to get enough of the blues and purples. The yardage listed is what I used for this particular fabric and includes some waste.

Not only does the raw-edge technique eliminate the necessity of sewing curved seams, in this quilt, the path pieces are sewn to the background-batting-backing quilt sandwich in fast quilt-as-you-go style—making this an even quicker project.

Finished Size

72" square before washing

Block Size

12"

Materials

4½ yards background black marbled fabric
4½ yards black backing fabric
2½ yards print "path" fabric
4½ yards or one queen-size batting
Quilting thread

Cutting Plan

From black background fabric, cut:
   Twenty-five 13" squares
   Four 8" x 61" border pieces
   Four 8" square border corner pieces
From the backing, cut:
   Twenty-five 13" squares
   Four 8" x 61" border pieces
   Four 8" square border corner pieces
From the batting, cut:
   Twenty-five 12" squares
   Four 6" x 60" border pieces
   Four 6" square border corner pieces
From the colored landscape fabric, cut:
   224 quarter-circle convex pieces
   104 concave pieces

Tip:

The seam allowances for this quilt are 1/4" for the colored "path" pieces and 1/2" for the seams used to sew the blocks and border sections together.

Tip:

Note that a 12" quilter's square and a 6" x 12" rotary-cutting ruler are used to mark the squares. Although not essential, these tools make the job quicker and easier.

Instructions

1 To mark the background squares, center a 12" ruler in the center of each square. Mark with a white pencil. Put aside twelve of these for the setting squares.

2 For the remaining thirteen squares, using a 6" x 12" ruler, draw a line down the center of the square and then side-to-side.

Center the middle 3" line of the 6" x 12" ruler over the lines you just marked, and then mark the edges.

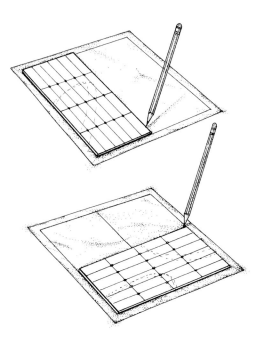

Step 1

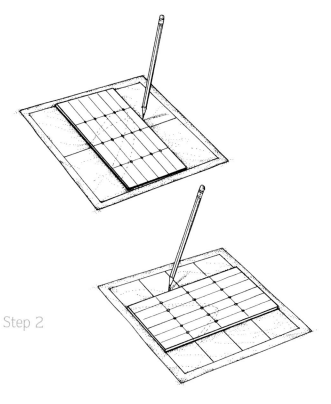

Step 2

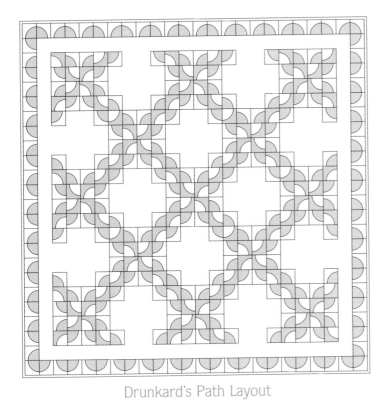

Drunkard's Path Layout

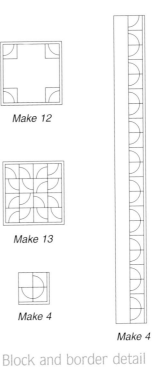

Make 12

Make 13

Make 4

Make 4

Block and border detail

3 Lay a background piece right-side down on your work surface. Center a piece of batting on top. Lay the marked background square, right-side up on top, matching edges. Safety pin.

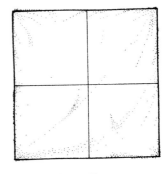

Step 3

4 Using a ¼" seam allowance, place, pin, and stitch the concave and convex path pieces to the background squares. Note that the seam allowances of the print fabric pieces will overlap the marked lines and each other ¼".

5 To mark the corner border background pieces, mark lines down the center of the block from top to bottom and side to side.

Step 5

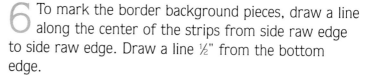

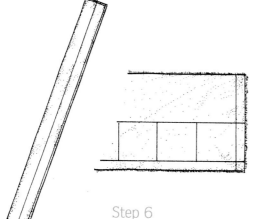

Step 6

6 To mark the border background pieces, draw a line along the center of the strips from side raw edge to side raw edge. Draw a line ½" from the bottom edge.

Draw a line ½" from both the left and right short edges. Mark vertical lines 3" apart in between the two lines as shown.

7 Layer the marked background pieces with backing and batting and safety pin the layers together.

8 Using a ¼" seam allowance, stitch the remaining concave path pieces to the sandwiched border sections.

9 Mark the quilt design, or trace onto freezer paper and iron on each block and the border sections. Quilt as shown at left.

Step 9

10 Arrange the blocks and border sections as they will appear in the finished quilt. Stand back from various angles to see how the color placement of the blocks works and rearrange until satisfied.

11 Using a ½" seam allowance and with backing sides facing, stitch the center into rows. Stitch the rows together.

12 Stitch the corner border sections to the ends of two border sections. Stitch the two remaining border sections to the sides of the quilt top. Stitch the border sections with the corner sections to the top and bottom of the quilt top.

13 Stitch ½" all the way around the outside edge of the quilting, stopping and starting at the seams.

Tip:
When you sew the rows together, and then when you stitch the borders on, you may elect to stitch right over the previous seam allowances, or you may skip and backstitch when you come to them, lift your presser foot, move past the seam allowances, and start stitching again.

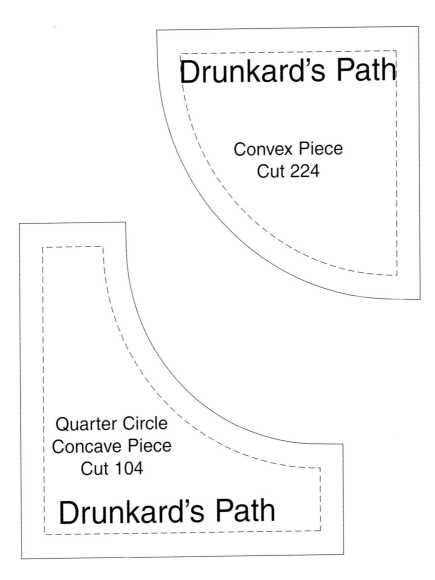

Drunkard's Path

Convex Piece
Cut 224

Quarter Circle
Concave Piece
Cut 104

Drunkard's Path

Orange Peel

What can I say about batiks?

One simply can't go wrong with them. They blend beautifully and turn any design into something special.

Of course, I simply had to choose oranges as my palette for a quilt of this name. And luckily, batiks offer delicious oranges.

Finished Size

54" square before washing

Materials

1¼ yards background fabric
⅓-yard orange 1 (A pieces)
⅔-yard orange 2 (B pieces)
1 yard orange 3 (C pieces)
¼-yard green inner border fabric
1 yard outer border fabric
¼-yard binding fabric
3 yards backing fabric

Cutting Plan

Cut the background fabric into a 42½" square.
Using the Orange Peel template on page 92, cut:
    Sixteen pieces from orange 1
    Thirty-six pieces from orange 2
    Forty-eight pieces from orange 3
Cut four 1½" strips of green fabric for the inner border.
Cut the outer border fabric into five 5½"-wide strips. (Sew sections of the fifth strip to the other four strips to make two 5½" x 44½" pieces for the side borders and two 5½" x 54½" pieces for the top and bottom borders.)
Cut six strips of binding 2½" wide from the green fabric.

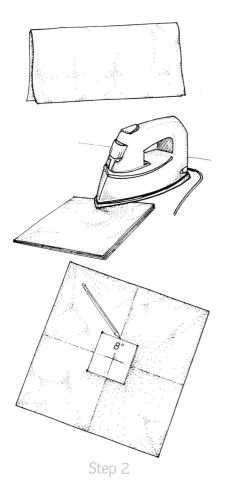

Instructions

1 To find and mark the center of the background fabric, fold it in half and in half again. Press the folds. Open up the fabric.

2 Using a rotary ruler and a pencil or blue washout pen, mark the quilt top into an 8" grid of squares. Start by centering the first 8" square at the intersection of the pressed lines and work out, using the pressed folds and preceding dots as guides marking the corners of the 8" squares. There is a 1" "float" of background outside the peel pieces.

3 Starting at the center, raw-edge appliqué the A pieces to the quilt top. Working out, appliqué the B pieces and then the C pieces. Use a ½" seam allowance.

Step 2

Step 3
Orange Peel Layout

4 Stitch green inner border strips to two sides of the quilt top. Trim to fit. Press seam allowances toward the strips. Repeat for the two remaining sides of the quilt.

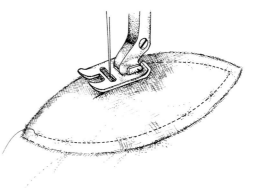

Step 4

5 Stitch the two 44½"-long outer border pieces to the sides of the quilt top. Press the seam allowances toward the outer border. Repeat for the top and bottom.

6 Using the templates provided on page 93, mark your quilt top for quilting.

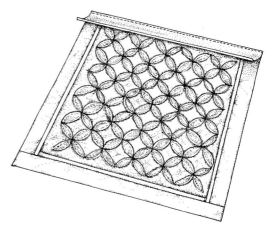

7 Cut the backing fabric into two 1½-yard pieces. Trim selvedges and seam the two pieces together along one set of selvedge edges, right sides facing. Press the seam allowances to one side.

8 Following the instructions on page 14, layer and baste your quilt sandwich together.

Step 5

9 Quilt your quilt using the quilting templates on page 93, as shown at right, or in your own design.

10 Seam the binding and bind your quilt as instructed on pages 16-17.

Step 9

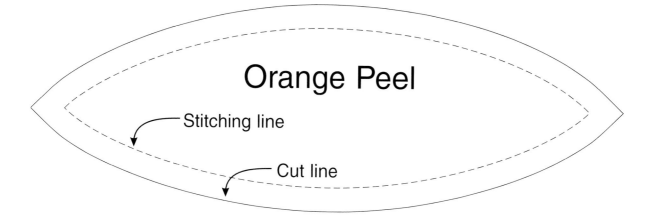

Orange Peel

Stitching line

Cut line

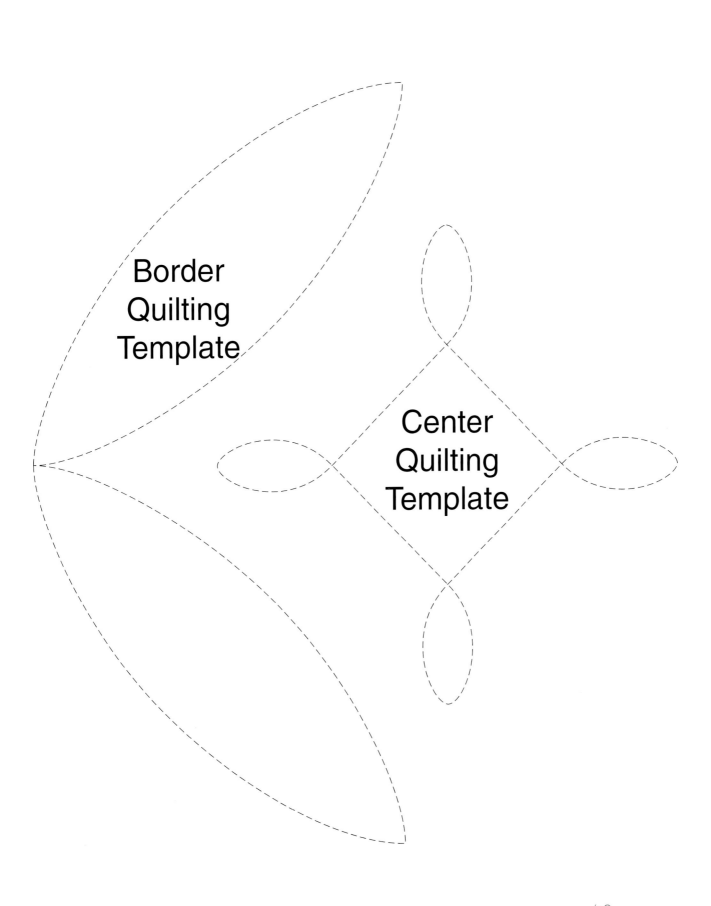

Border
Quilting
Template

Center
Quilting
Template

Sources

Theresa's Hand Dyed Buttons
Hillcreek Designs
(619) 562-5799

These are the buttons I used for Orange Peel. If they are not available at your local quilt shop, call the number above.

Mail-Order Shopping

Nothing beats visiting a quilt shop to see all the latest luscious fabrics and sewn samples, not to mention the camaraderie of being with fellow quilt lovers. Believe me, I help the local shops thrive.

But there is never enough fabric and quilting goodies for my appetite, so I often use mail-order and online quilting sources.

Here are the resources I use and recommend each of them without hesitation.

Catalog Shopping

Keepsake Quilting
Route 25B
P.O. Box 1618
Centre Harbor, NH 03226-1618
(800) 865-9458
Call for a free catalog.
www.keepsakequilting.com

A beefy little catalog, chock-full of all the latest and tried-and-true quilt notions, gadgets, patterns, books, and fabric and handy fabric medleys, too. It is no wonder Keepsake is entitled, "The Quilter's Wishbook!"

Connecting Threads
P.O. Box 8940
Vancouver, WA 98668-8940
(800) 574-6454
Call for a free catalog.
www.connectingthreads.com

This catalog is a quilting education in itself. See what's available, what's new, and what's hot. Also check out the recently launched Connecting Threads Web site, which is full of books, patterns, fabrics, and most every quilting tool imaginable—all at discounted prices.

Hancock's of Paducah

Hancock's of Paducah
3841 Hinkleville Road
Paducah, KY 42001
(800) 845-8723
www.Hancocks-Paducah.com

Fabric and more fabric is the focus in this delicious catalog. The latest fabrics from the best manufacturers and designers, plus threads, quilting gadgets, batting, and more—all at great prices—are featured here. Check out both the online and paper catalogs since one may have fabrics the other doesn't.

Nancy's Notions®
1-800-833-0690

Nancy's Notions
P.O. Box 683
Beaver Dam, WI 53916
(800) 833-0690
www.nancysnotions.com

The Sew Steady table I bought for my Bernina extends my work surface and also doubles as a light box as it is made of Plexiglass. They are available in stock and custom sizes.

Quilts & Other Comforts
1 Quilters Lane
P.O. Box 4100
Golden, CO 80401-0100
(800) 881-6624
Call for a free catalog.

Focusing on fabrics and patterns, "The catalog for quilt lovers" features a good selection of the most popular books and all those wonderful quilt tools as well. You'll find some nice quilty gift-type items, too.

Online Shopping

Bighorn Quilts
608 Greybull Ave.
P.O. Box 566
Greybull, WY 82426
(877) 586-9150
www.bighornquilts.com

Fabric certainly does take center stage here at "The World Wide Online Fabric Store." And there is lots of it—all at I-can't-resist prices.

PINETREE QUILTWORKS, LTD.

Pine Tree Quiltworks, Ltd.
585 Broadway
South Portland, ME 04107
(207) 799-7357
www.quiltworks.com
Or call for a free catalog.

Bring up this site for a complete online
quilt shop, including a wonderful
selection of fabrics and every ruler
and other notion imaginable, all at
discounted prices.

Quilt-a-way Fabrics
540 Back Westminster Road
Westminster, VT 05150
(802) 722-4743
www.quiltaway.com

A full-service quilt shop, Quilt-a-way's
mail-order site offers a great
selection of fabrics at the lowest
possible prices, including many batiks.

eQuilter
4581 Maple Court
Boulder, CO 80301
(303) 516-1615
www.eQuilter.com

You'll find a huge number of fabrics
arranged by theme here and lots
of batiks, including some exclusives,
as well as all sorts of interesting
fabrics—quilting and otherwise.

Gammill Quilting Systems

Gammill Quilting Systems
www.gammill.net

Here, you will find the Rose Vine design
used to quilt Rose Log Cabin.

Online Resources

Here are a few starting points for
exploring quilting and foundation piecing
in the wonderful world of cyberspace.

Judy Smith's Quilting, Needlearts and Antiques Page

Judy Smith's Quilting, Needlearts and
Antiques Page
www.quiltart.com/judy

Judy is an online quilter from way back
and has a highly acclaimed site of
great quilting links. Starting your
search with Judy's site, you'll quickly
accrue a long list of bookmarked
favorites!

About.com
www.quilting.about.com

The mission of About.com is to be the
place to go to learn about any topic.
Each site is devoted to a specific
area of interest and is hosted by a
real, live, accessible human being.
And Susan Druding's Quilting site
does just that. It's a resource for all
facets of quilting, offering how-tos,
FAQs, sources, links to other sites,
and much, much more.

Planet Patchwork
www.planetpatchwork.com

Find links to lessons, patterns, people,
and more here. With the rich
content of this site, take a virtual
tour of a quilt shop, meet a growing
number of well-known quilters, read
book reviews, and find great prices
on quilting software.

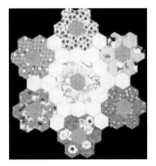

Quilt Net
www.quilt.net

You'll find a plethora of links here.

The Quilt Channel

The Quilt Channel
www.quiltchannel.com

Find shops, guilds, and a whole lot more
at this site.

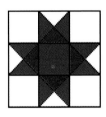

The World Wide Quilting Page
http://ttsw.com/MainQuiltingPage.html

Check this site out for links to quilt-
related e-mail lists. These are
commonly called "online guilds,"
which is an apt description. Imagine
conversing with quilters from all
over the country—and world!

Meet the Author

Jodie Davis has written more than two dozen craft books. Lately, she has focused on quilting, in such titles as *Hometown Quilts, Paper-Piece a Flower Garden,* and *Paper-Pieced Curves.* She is known for being innovative and "clever" and reports that her raw-edge appliqué quilts are the most fun she's ever had making quilts—and she's been doing it a long time!

Originally from Rhode Island, Jodie now enjoys the climate and the Southern hospitality of her new home in Georgia.

When she's not immersed in her latest quilting project or book, Jodie and her husband, Bill Barthlow, are avid gardeners who often can be found weeding and pruning while their feline friends "help."

Not one to be left out on the collecting scene, Jodie's rubber ducky collection has attracted much publicity. More than 300 of her yellow buddies reside in the bathroom adjacent to her studio— ever an inspiration to her creative and playful side.

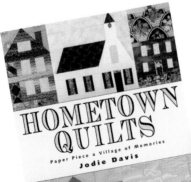

Also by Jodie Davis

Crafting Lamps & Shades and *Hometown Quilts* are available from Krause Publications, too. Please call (800) 258-0929 or visit www.krause.com for information.